FOR A GOOD TIME

FOR A GOOD TIME

SURVIVING SEX WORK AND ADDICTION TO BECOME
THE MOTHER I WAS MEANT TO BE

PATTY TIERNEY

SHE WRITES PRESS

Published 2022
Printed in the United States of America
Print ISBN: 978-1-64742-289-9
E-ISBN: 978-1-64742-290-5
Library of Congress Control Number: 2022905826

For information, address:
She Writes Press
1569 Solano Ave #546
Berkeley, CA 94707

She Writes Press is a division of SparkPoint Studio, LLC.

All company and/or product names may be trade names, logos, trademarks, and/or registered trademarks and are the property of their respective owners.

Names and identifying characteristics have been changed to protect the privacy of certain individuals. The author has purposely left interior letters verbatim and unedited.

I dedicate this book to all the mothers who just want to be good moms.

I pray that you may find strength and hope through the power of forgiveness.

Contents

Foreword

The first time I ever saw Patty Tierney, I cried. I had no idea who she was, or that she was going to be there that day. But right in that moment, my friend whispered in my ear.

"Oh, I forgot to tell you, Patty was a prostitute," she said nonchalantly as she pointed across the room.

It was 2013, I was twenty-nine years old, and my life had been a mess. I had just decided to quit my job as a sex worker and was having a hard time finding new work. I had lived a lifetime of being depressed, hopeless, and suicidal, and I was self-destructing in my addictions. My boyfriend at the time still had no idea what I had been doing behind his back.

We were at something called Goddess Camp, an event that my friend promised me would change my life. "A bunch of women teach you how to love yourself," she told me. I had confessed to her the double life I had been living, and the event just so happened to be that weekend, so she invited me. "WE'RE GOING" was all I texted her. I was completely desperate at that point.

After the initial disbelief that my friend had never told me about Patty, I felt the powerful feeling of there being someone in the room who understood me, someone who knew what I had been through.

For the first time, I didn't feel alone. I just couldn't stop crying, and I hadn't even met her yet.

After I shared my story with the whole room, everyone directed me toward Patty. I sobbed for hours as she held me to her chest. I asked her over and over again, through tears, if it was really possible for me to love myself and be happy. And over and over again, she reassured me that I could have everything I wanted and more.

Since that day, my life has changed completely. Patty and her husband, John, have guided me to self-love, acceptance, forgiveness, and truth. For every challenge I've faced, every fire I've walked through, every victory, every triumph, Patty has been there. She is like the mother I always wanted but never had—which is why, to this day, I call her my spirit mom.

When I first read this book, I couldn't believe all of the things Patty had been through in her life and how far she'd come to get to where she is now. It is one of the most amazing, compelling, courageous, brave, inspiring, empowering stories I've ever heard. If you met Patty today, you would never guess that she'd been through everything she's been through. Patty is the happiest, most joyful, and most grateful person I know. She has taught me that love is all that matters, that feeling good is why we're here, and that it doesn't matter what other people think. She inspires me to stand in my power, dream big, believe, and trust the journey. It is because of her that I'm still alive today. It is because of her that all I want to do is help others and change the world, just like she does. And it is because of her that I will never judge a person by what's on the outside—Patty is beautiful proof that you just never know what a person's story is.

I am thrilled for the world to read her story and feel as inspired by her as I am.

—Charlene deGuzman

Chapter One
The Cardboard House

"Where's my mommy?!" I cried.

It was a winter evening in 1953 in Altadena, California. I was five years old. My older brothers, Steve and Greg, were six and eight. Greg didn't seem worried that our mother hadn't been home in two days. He only cared about watching Superman on TV. But I was worried. Terribly worried.

"I want my mommy!" I shouted.

"Stop it, Patty! I don't know where she is!" Greg yelled.

"You'll be okay," Steve assured me. "Mommy will be home soon." Steve wasn't mean like Greg.

"She wasn't home when I woke up this morning," I told him.

"Maybe she didn't look at the clock," Steve said. "Come on."

He took my hand and led me to the kitchen, where he made us peanut butter and jelly sandwiches and served them on my tea set. We ate them like they were the best things we'd ever tasted. When we were finished, we left the plates on the floor and went outside to play.

Steve was giving me piggyback rides up and down our driveway when two bright beams of light shot through the night.

Terrified, we ran toward the door of our house and stopped short at the sound of a man's deep voice.

"Do you kids live here?"

I spun around to see a police officer. Behind him were the bright lights on top of his car.

"Maybe Mommy's in there!" I cried, tugging at Steve's arm.

The officer shook his head. "She's not in there. I'm looking for her. Is she home?"

"No!" Steve and I chorused.

Greg came outside while Steve and I stood frozen.

"Did the neighbors call you?" asked Greg. "They keep coming over and asking where my mom is."

"And do you know where she is?" the officer asked.

"I have no idea," Greg replied.

"It's too cold out here with bare feet," the officer said, ushering us inside.

We followed Greg through the living room and to the kitchen table, where he moved open boxes of cereal onto the crowded counter and wiped away spilled milk. The officer pulled up a chair and took out a notepad.

"Does anyone live here besides your mother?" the officer asked.

"Nope," said Greg.

The officer scribbled. "Where is your father?" he asked.

"She's divorced. He doesn't live in this state," Greg told him.

He scribbled again. "What does your mother look like?"

"She has red fingernails," I offered.

"She has dark hair, and her eyes are blue," Greg told him. "She's not fat or skinny, and she's not short or tall."

"Very good." He scribbled again. "What was she wearing when you last saw her?"

"A black skirt, a white blouse that buttons up the back, and black shoes," Steve chimed in.

The officer looked over at the empty beer bottles on the kitchen counter. "Does your mom have a boyfriend?"

"She has a few of them," said Greg.

This time he didn't scribble.

"Has your mother called?" he asked.

"Our phone doesn't work," said Greg. "Mom didn't pay the bill."

The officer stood up, the legs of his chair scraping the linoleum.

"Kids," he said, "we're going somewhere you can stay while we look for your mother."

"We can stay here," Steve insisted.

"What if you don't find her?" asked Greg.

"We'll find her," the officer said, sounding certain they would. He took my hand in his. I looked over my shoulder at Steve.

"Where are you taking her?" asked Steve.

"I'm taking all of you to juvenile hall. There are kids there just like you," he told us.

Just like us?

"I want to stay here!" I cried, bursting into tears. "How will my mommy find me?"

The officer put his big hands on my shoulders and crouched down.

"You'll find out the minute we find your mom," he said. His voice was gentler now, but I couldn't stop crying. Leave home? Maybe never see my mom again? What if they forgot to tell me when she came home?

Greg came back carrying his coat and my fluffy pink coat with the white muff collar. Steve took a jacket from the pile of clothes on the couch, and we fell into step behind the officer.

In the back of the police car, Greg scowled with folded arms. He kicked the back of the officer's seat, then rocked back and forth for the whole ride, slamming his back on the seat over and over again. I hugged my coat tight and buried my face in it.

The police car pulled up in front of a big brick building, and we followed the officer inside. A small woman in a yellow plastic apron greeted us.

"You must be Patty," she said.

I nodded without looking up and moved closer to Steve.

"I'm Mrs. Martinez." She reached for my hand. "Say goodbye for now to your brothers. You're going to the girls' side."

"No!" I screamed.

"You'll see them tomorrow," she said, pulling me in her direction.

"Bye, Patty," said Steve. "Don't cry."

His teeth were chattering. Greg didn't say a word.

The next thing I knew, I was being told to take off my clothes and climb into a bathtub. After my bath, I was dressed in blue pajamas.

I was led down a long, dimly lit corridor by a big woman in a tan uniform. She stopped in front of a door and unhooked the big key ring that dangled from her belt loop.

"You'll stay here tonight," she said flatly. We entered a small room containing only a bed. "It's late, and we don't want to disturb the other girls."

I was frozen.

"It's late!" she snapped. "Go on and get to sleep."

I started to cry again. I climbed into bed. She closed the door and locked it. Her footsteps retreated down the hall.

Why had I been taken from my brothers and locked in this prison cell? I hadn't done anything wrong.

It felt like hours had passed when I got out of bed and pounded on the door with both fists. "I want my mommy! I want my mommy!" I sobbed. No one came.

Finally, the woman with the keys unlocked the door. "Now, you know you shouldn't be crying like this!" she scolded. "You'll wake the other girls. Stop crying and get back in bed."

I sucked in my breath. "Don't lock me in. I'll stop crying if you leave the door open just a tiny bit."

She gave in and said, "Just a crack."

I listened to the clanging of keys as the woman disappeared down the hall. Maybe I had done something wrong, I worried. Maybe my mom was horribly mad at me. Maybe she didn't want to come and get me. Maybe she didn't want to be my mom anymore! I lay there and quietly cried myself to sleep.

The next morning, there was a knock on my door. "Wake up, Patty!" A new woman peeked inside. Her name was Miss Rose.

I sat up quickly. Maybe Miss Rose was nicer than the lady with the clanging keys.

"I'm taking you to meet the other girls," said Miss Rose.

I took Miss Rose's hand, and she led me to a big gray room lined with perfectly made beds.

"You'll be happy here," said Miss Rose. "There are nine girls between the ages of four and twelve. You'll fit right in."

She showed me to my new bed and introduced me to the little girl sitting on the bed beside it. "This is Jenny. She's five too."

Jenny and I looked at each other. Miss Rose helped us get dressed in the pretty slips, dresses, and socks at the ends of our beds. She brushed Jenny's brown hair into two short pigtails.

"You look adorable, Jenny," she said.

She brushed my blonde hair, smiling. "Look at you, with those Shirley Temple curls. You're precious!"

Jenny and I held hands as we stood in line for breakfast. We sat at a long table and ate oatmeal, scrambled eggs, buttered toast, and sliced oranges. We talked nonstop, and by the time breakfast was over, Jenny and I were best friends.

Then Miss Rose brought all of us girls to the coed schoolroom.

I was coloring when I saw Greg and Steve walk in. I sprang out of my chair and ran to them, throwing my arms around them. Even Greg said it was good to see me.

Suddenly, Miss Rose asked us to come with her. We followed her to her office and sat down.

"Your mother's home," Miss Rose told us. "Safe and sound."

I clapped my hands.

"Where was she?" asked Greg.

"With a friend. She said she was sick. But she's fine now, and she's coming on Sunday."

"Oh, boy!" I shouted. "When is Sunday?"

"In five days," said Greg, not smiling.

And that was all there was to it. Our mom was home again, our meeting was done, and it was time to go outside and play.

All week long, I played. Jenny and I were inseparable. I couldn't wait to tell my mom about her, Miss Rose, and all of the other kids. I hoped she wasn't sick anymore.

When Sunday finally came, Miss Rose walked in with our mom.

"Mommy!" we shouted, running to her.

She looked pretty with her short dark hair, green dress, string of pearls, and long coat. I couldn't take my eyes off her. She pulled off her tight gloves one finger at a time, revealing one beautifully polished red fingernail after the next. She wrapped her arms around all of us and drew us close. Tears ran down her face, but I couldn't hear her crying.

"What's wrong?" I asked. "Are you still sick? You don't seem sick."

"That means I must be getting better. I've missed you so much," she said with a sigh, wiping her eyes.

"Why do you drink if it makes you sick?" asked Greg.

"I don't know," she said, hugging us tighter. "Sometimes I forget what I'm doing."

I didn't understand. Alcohol was something my mom rubbed on my chest when I had a fever. It would taste awful. No wonder she felt sick.

She shook her head. "I'm so, so sorry. I didn't mean to be gone so long."

Greg glared at her. "You should come home when you're supposed to!"

"I took care of Patty," Steve offered.

Our mother cried even harder.

"Can we go home now?" I asked.

"Not today," she said. "I had to go to court. The judge said you could be taken away from me permanently if I don't quit drinking. I have to go back to court in three days. I'll come back and see you next Sunday, I promise."

My stomach felt like it was sitting on the floor. I looked around for Jenny.

"I love you so much," she told us.

Our mother came back the next Sunday. It was finally time to go home. I was sad to leave my friends, especially Jenny. She had no plans to go home. We cried saying goodbye.

Our house was located in a nice, mostly residential neighborhood of Pasadena; it was a small two-bedroom with a backyard. The house was behind some office buildings and had been used as a communication station during World War II. Bamboo grew in the yard, and we liked to sharpen the ends of bamboo poles and pretend they were spears. If the tip accidentally hit the house, it pierced the wall a good two inches. Mom told us that our house was made out of cardboard.

Before Pasadena, we lived in Phoenix, Arizona, where I was born. Mom divorced Dad when I was two years old and decided to move to California. She heard that single mothers could get a monthly welfare check here. Maybe she didn't think she could support us by herself, or maybe she wanted to be at home with us all day, or maybe she just didn't want to work. All I know is that we moved to California and lived on welfare. And I hated it. All of my friends' parents worked, but not my mom. My brothers and I looked in the mailbox every day so we could get the checks before anyone discovered our secret.

I don't remember my father. Mom didn't talk about him much. All I knew about him was that he was tall, dark, and handsome; he played bass in a big band; and he had a small part in the movie *Springtime in the Rockies*. It was on TV once and if I didn't blink, I could catch a glimpse of him. Mom said he was gone a lot, traveling with his band, and that had caused a lot of problems in their marriage.

It was good to be home. For nearly two years after our stay in juvenile hall, our mom took care of us. She walked us to school. She helped us with our homework. She cooked dinner every night. Sunday night was fried chicken night. Wednesday night was family night and Mom played badminton and horseshoes with us in the backyard. We played games like Doggy, Doggy, Who Has Your Bone? and Red Light, Green Light. Maybe things got a lot better for us because of the judge's warning, or maybe it was because my mother wasn't drinking as much.

On Sunday mornings we walked the few blocks to church, and sometimes I invited a friend home to play before we went back to church again in the evening. I was always nervous about bringing a friend home. Mormons weren't supposed to drink or smoke, and I knew Mom did both. I would hide the ashtrays and put any beer bottles behind the milk.

Church was a big part of our lives, but I didn't really believe in God. If my mom didn't practice the church teachings, wasn't everything associated with church a lie? I thought everyone was faking it when they said they believed in God, and I faked it along with them.

One day, when I was in the first grade, my dad called. He said that he loved me and he wanted to come see me. He came over and brought me a doll. But after that visit, I never saw him again.

I missed having a dad and thought there was something wrong with me since everyone else had a dad. But at the same time, I was glad I didn't have one because I thought that all they did was punish their kids.

One night, my mom told me and my brothers a story about the time in her life before she was married to our dad, before we were born. She'd been married to another man, and they'd had a beautiful daughter named Gloria, a little girl with curly brown hair. When Gloria was eleven, she asked to go to the movies with a couple of girlfriends. Mom told Gloria she was too young to go without an adult, but her girlfriends promised they would be fine. They begged; the theater was only a few blocks away. Finally, Mom agreed to let them go as long as they stayed close together.

On the way to the theater, Gloria's girlfriends ran across the street at a yellow traffic light. When they reached the other side, they called to Gloria. "Come on! You can make it! Run!" Gloria started across the street at the exact moment a truck came around the corner. The truck hit her and she went flying, landing facedown on the pavement. The girls ran to tell Mom, who arrived in time to see her critically injured daughter lying in the street. Little Gloria died on the way to the hospital.

Mom was shattered. Her grief was unbearable. She blamed herself for not listening to her intuition, which had told her, *You shouldn't let her go.* She never drove a car again. She divorced Gloria's dad and, a few years later, married our dad and had three more children.

And she started to drink. She told us we were too young to understand.

I loved being with my mother when she wasn't drinking. The summer I was seven, we would walk three blocks to the library to check out books. We chose books for me, and she checked out books for herself. She read a lot when she wasn't drinking.

The happiest days were when Mom took me to swimming lessons at the YWCA. It was time for just us, special time. Mom sewed my guppy and tadpole badges on the front of my suit. And she always sat in the balcony to watch my lessons. When I got into the pool, the first thing I'd do was look up to the balcony to make sure she was watching. I'd call out and wave, "Hi, Mom!" and it would echo. Mom would stand and wave back like she was seeing me for the first time. I was so proud.

After the lessons, we'd stop at the drugstore and Mom would buy me Life Savers candy to eat on the walk home while we talked. I'd tell her I still liked Stuart, my boyfriend since the first grade. "That's so nice, honey. He's such a nice boy," Mom would tell me.

Summers were especially hot in the cardboard house. My brothers and I rode our bikes around the neighborhood and played in our treehouse. Some nights, Mom let us take our beds into the backyard to sleep. We listened to the crickets chirp as we gazed up at the stars. I loved this time outdoors with my brothers. Life was good.

And then things began to change.

Chapter Two
Dumb, Stupid Girl

"When is my mommy coming home?" I asked the operator. "It's dark outside. I'm hungry."

"Don't worry, honey, I'm sure your mommy will be home in a few minutes," she told me. Mom was drinking again. She was back at the bars, staying out late. I was seven years old. I called the operator whenever she wasn't home by dinnertime. When she finally did come home, her breath smelled like beer. She was different. I felt sad and afraid that something awful was going to happen. It usually did when her breath smelled like beer.

Early one morning, my brothers and I woke up to see a man's shirt draped over the back of the couch. In the kitchen there was an empty quart of beer next to a mountain of cigarette butts. We just stood there, staring at each other. Greg motioned for us to follow him. We peeked through Mom's slightly open bedroom door to see her in bed with a man on top of her. I felt left out. *I always sleep with Mommy*, I thought. *Why is that man in my bed?*

We would eventually find out that this was Victor, a friend from a neighborhood bar. He had wavy dark hair, olive skin, a medium build, and he was kind of short. Victor returned night after night to sit in our kitchen, get drunk with Mom, and spend the night. Mom didn't pay attention to us. In fact, she acted like we weren't even there. I felt abandoned, like I didn't matter anymore. Victor didn't talk to us much either, but we weren't interested anyway.

Every night and all weekend, they drank beer and smoked cigarettes, went to bars, and came home late. Mom didn't cook dinner for us anymore. There were no more fried chicken Sundays or family night Wednesdays. We stopped going to church. I never went to the library. If I needed a dress ironed for school, I ironed it myself. I felt sad and wished I had a nice family like my friends did. I was ashamed of my family. My family was nothing like my friends' families.

Sometimes my brothers and I would pour full bottles of beer down the kitchen sink, hoping it would help. It never did. They always came home with new bottles. I felt abandoned by my mom. I hated the way she cared about Victor and not me at all.

The next year, Victor moved in with us. That was the same year Mom and Victor started fighting. One time, my mom cracked a beer bottle over Victor's head, and he punched her. I hid behind the couch, shaking, as I stared at Victor, blood running down his face. I was terrified. I thought someone was going to die.

That was the day I cut myself off from my emotions because I had no control. If I had emotions, I'd have to feel scared, worried, and helpless. I never felt safe at home again. I thought we were the only people who lived like this. I thought I came from trash.

My brothers and I tried to make Victor leave, but it never worked. We called the cops when the fights got really bad, and Victor would be taken to jail. But because Mom never wanted to press charges, they always released him the next day. This went on for years.

Terrified that I could be taken away from Mom again, I was on alert, and I was sure that if anyone argued, or even raised their voices, it would lead to an argument, which would eventually turn violent.

This was when the people pleaser in me was born. I was afraid to upset anyone. If everyone was happy, I'd be safe.

Sometimes, when Victor was too drunk to stand up, my brothers and I grabbed him and threw him down on a mattress. We wrapped the telephone cord around his arms and legs and shook salt and pepper onto him. But the fights continued. For eight years, I never felt safe at home again.

* * *

Despite the chaos in our home, my brothers and I got ourselves to school—for the most part. Greg always got good grades, and I did okay, but Steve often pretended to be sick so he wouldn't have to go. When it was time for Steve to begin eighth grade, he finally just stopped going to school altogether. Because Mom was drunk so much, she didn't seem to care. Steve was always smart, but he was happier staying home and building ham radios or tinkering with something electronic. The truant officers never came around to make him return. I always wished they had.

Steve was my ally and my support. No matter how bad it was, he always said, "It'll be all right, Patty. You'll be okay." Once, Greg was my ally too—I was eight and some of my Brownies troop was going to summer camp. I wanted more than anything to go, but Mom didn't have enough money. Greg saw how disappointed I was and surprised me.

"Patty," he said, "I saved some of my paper route money. Take it and go to camp." I threw my arms around him and told him he was the best brother in the world. I ended up loving camp—swimming, hiking, crafts, and songs around the campfire. And s'mores! Though I missed my family and friends, especially my boyfriend, Stuart, I didn't miss the way things were at home.

After summer camp ended, I brought my girlfriend, Barbara, home to see our treehouse. We were walking up the driveway when all of a sudden, my mom burst out of the house naked, with Victor chasing her. My heart felt like it was beating out of my chest. I panicked and grabbed Barbara's shoulders to turn her around.

"Wait!" I shouted. "I just remembered I'm not supposed to bring anyone home to play on Saturdays. But I can play at your house!"

I took Barbara's hand and dragged her down the block. All I could think about were the horrible things that were going to happen to my mom when Victor got her.

Another day, Barbara and I were kicking up leaves that covered the sidewalk in front of her house. I noticed a public mailbox and got an idea.

"Let's see if we can fill this mailbox up to the top!" I exclaimed. We took turns stuffing leaves into the mailbox until it was full. But someone must have seen us and called the police, and soon an officer arrived and we were lectured on destroying public property. The police escorted us both home and told our parents. My mom looked right at me.

"You're a dumb, stupid girl," she slurred. I didn't say anything. Her words cut me to the core. She may have only said them once, but they would play over and over in my head for years. At some point, I believed them.

I may have bought into what my mom said, that I was a dumb, stupid girl, but I was smart enough to know that if I lifted up my top, I could get what I wanted.

One day that fall, I was with my brothers and a few of the neighborhood boys at Woolworth's drugstore. "I have a surprise for you, wait here," I said, and I went into the fifty-cent photo booth. I made silly faces while holding my T-shirt pulled all the way up. I was bold, and

I wanted the boys to know it. They always left me behind when they'd take off riding their bikes, and I didn't want to be stuck at home with my mom and Victor and without my brothers because I never knew when a fight would break out. I thought the photos would make the boys pay attention to me at least. I was the youngest in the group. And I was a girl. When I showed them the pictures, their faces turned red with embarrassment. But from then on, they let me ride with them. I didn't know it yet, but this was my first glimpse of my superpower.

* * *

My mom had been ordered by the court to attend AA meetings. But she didn't believe she was an alcoholic. One day, when it was time to attend her AA meeting down the street, she left the house with a bottle of Ripple in her purse. My brothers and I tried to talk her out of going, but she was headstrong.

"I'm going to the meeting," she told us. "I'll give them something better than coffee with their cookies!"

We didn't want Mom to be arrested, so we tagged along with her, thinking we could prevent it. We waited in the lobby, where we could see everything. Mom heckled the speaker.

"Way to go!" she shouted. "You tell 'em, Bob!"

After the meeting, Mom went up to a man standing near the refreshments table and showed him her wine bottle. "You'd rather have some Ripple, now, wouldn't you?"

We didn't want anyone to call the police, so we stepped in.

"Come on, Mom. Let's go home," Greg said.

I swore I'd never drink when I grew up. I'd be the best mom in the world. My kids would have a good life. I had no idea my mom's behavior was giving me a sense of worthlessness that would affect my future in ways I never could have dreamed.

And that future started the summer after seventh grade, the day my girlfriend JoAnne and I stole a half pint of vodka from Thrifty Drug Store. JoAnne and I took the bottle of vodka and a six-pack of Coke to a local park, mixed the vodka into a couple of cans, and started drinking. We drank and laughed until we got sick and threw up.

Sometimes JoAnne and I shoplifted for the thrill of it—a record album, a candy bar. I was acting out, and why not? I could get away with it. I never got grounded, and I could come and go as I pleased. One day, I asked my mother why I was never grounded.

"All my friends get grounded," I insisted.

"You don't have to be like everybody else," she told me. I wanted to get grounded. I wanted her to care enough to ground me.

Greg was acting out too. One night, he took our landlord's car for a joyride and was caught. We were evicted. The only reason we had been able to stay in the cardboard house for seven years was because the nearest house was several lots away and the neighbors couldn't hear all the noise.

Over the next four years, we moved twenty-three times. That's an average of six times a year. Our frequent evictions resulted either from the noise of my mother's fights or because we couldn't pay the rent. I felt anxious and fearful through all this trauma. I was so ashamed of who we were, the way we lived.

Mom was sober sometimes, for as long as three months at a time. During those drinking breaks, she worked as a waitress and collected a paycheck. I always hoped it would last, even though her sobriety brought a new set of problems. My mother was nervous when she was sober. It didn't take much to upset her. Sometimes she got so upset with us that she would start shaking all over, fall to the floor, and foam at the mouth. We swore that we would never make her mad again. But then it would happen again. And each time it did, we blamed ourselves.

I was the one to blame the day I took Steve shoplifting at a nice department store. Steve had never shoplifted and didn't really want to. But I practically begged him to go with me. I wanted to show him how I did it. I had a big basket purse with a scarf draped over the top.

"Watch how easy it is," I said as we sauntered through the crowded first floor. We arrived at the watch department, where I picked up a small windup alarm clock and put it in my purse. "That's it," I said. "Done."

We left the store, but in moments, a plainclothes cop put a hand on my shoulder. Busted. Steve and I were put into a police car. Steve was quiet the whole way to the police station, and I could barely look at him. I pleaded to the officer that Steve hadn't done a thing. The officer said Steve was just as guilty because he was with me. But when we got to the station, the officer just told us not to do it again, and, thankfully, he let us go.

Not long after this happened, JoAnne and I were invited to a special dress-up party at a girlfriend's house. We both needed a pair of pantyhose to wear, but neither of us had any money to buy them. We had a girlfriend who could sign on her mother's account at the department store, so JoAnne pretended to be her and signed for the pantyhose. While we waited for the cashier to finish the transaction, the phone rang and the cashier picked it up. She hesitated in handing us the pantyhose, then started to look around the store, as if she was expecting to see someone.

"Run!" I shouted at JoAnne, and I ran as fast as I could. In no time, a plainclothes cop caught us. This time I wasn't so lucky. We were in trouble for forgery. JoAnne and I were sentenced to one week in juvenile hall. I served my time, and I never stole again.

In the eighth grade, I had my first real boyfriend, Roger. (Stuart had moved away.) He was good-looking, the quarterback of the football team, and one of the most popular guys at school, but I couldn't believe he liked me. I always thought he was fooled. I believed that if he really knew me, he wouldn't like me. I didn't think I deserved a guy who came from a good family. I was convinced I wasn't good enough for him. It was too good to be true.

Several of my girlfriends were cheerleaders, and I wanted to join the squad, but I didn't have the grades to try out. I was so busy trying to stay away from home that I didn't do my homework, and I was bored in most of my classes because I didn't keep up. I usually talked and passed notes, and I was sometimes asked to stand in the hall so I wouldn't disrupt class.

In my math class, however, I tried hard to catch up. I didn't like being behind, so I decided to pay attention and ask questions. One day, I raised my hand, feeling like part of the class. The teacher called on me, and I asked him to clarify something I didn't understand.

"Patty," he said, "if you had bothered to read the assignment and do the homework, you wouldn't be asking such a ridiculous question."

That was it. I was a dumb, stupid girl. I felt like an idiot. I was embarrassed. I vowed never to raise my hand in class again. This moment sharply defined my life.

* * *

One day when I came home from school, I could tell by the looks of things that Mom and Victor had had another big fight. The lamps were knocked over in their bedroom, and the stuff in Mom's purse was thrown all over the place; even her money and change were strewn everywhere. Mom was gone, and when I walked by the bathroom, Victor was standing in front of the mirror cutting his chest and stomach with a razor blade. He was bleeding profusely. My heart raced. I got the hell out of there.

I wondered if Mom was beat up. Was she okay? It made me sick to see them the very next day sitting in the kitchen drinking beer as if nothing had happened. I hated that they never remembered when they had been fighting.

At the time, I was fifteen, Steve was seventeen, and Greg was nineteen. Greg was big enough to do something about Victor, and he'd finally had enough. So a few days later, in the middle of one of Mom and Victor's fights, Greg grabbed Victor and dragged him outside. Mom, Steve, and I cheered from the front porch as Greg beat up Victor in the gravel parking lot next door. Steve and I gathered Victor's clothes from inside and threw them on him, yelling, "Don't ever come back!"

Victor picked up his clothes and staggered away. He was gone, at last. But as it turned out, Victor's departure didn't mean the end of our troubles. No more than five minutes after Victor left, Mom grabbed her purse.

"See you later," she said. And she headed for her favorite bar.

Chapter Three
A Boyfriend and a Best Friend

"Come here, Patty!" Steve shouted. "I think they're talking about Mom!"

Steve had built a police scanner. He would order kits to build all kinds of electronics and became quite the expert. He never had to pay for these kits because we'd move again by the time the bill came. I squeezed into the closet that was Steve's bedroom and sat beside him.

"What do you mean?" I asked him.

"The police are talking about a drunk lady dressed in an orange muumuu in the park around the corner," he explained. "Listen." He held up the scanner and we leaned in.

Steve showed up at the police station just in time to convince the officers to let my mom go. The thought of her alone and wandering around drunk scared my sixteen-year-old mind. I worried they might have thrown her in jail.

The next morning, Mom sat at the kitchen table like a zombie. I told her about what had happened with Steve's scanner.

"What are you talking about?" she asked indignantly.

"Yesterday, when the police picked you up in the park. That's how Steve found you," I explained.

"I wasn't in any park," she retorted. Mom never remembered her drunk incidents. "Fine then," Mom said.

She pulled a bottle of wine out of the cupboard, unscrewed the cap, and poured herself a glass. "Anyone heard the weather report?"

Steve walked in rolling his eyes and poured himself a glass of wine too.

I watched them with a sinking stomach. This was my family.

Years earlier, Steve had promised me he was never going to drink. He wasn't even going to try it. Everything changed when a friend of his gave him a wine-making kit for Christmas. At first he did it just to see how the wine tasted. Now he was drinking every day with Mom. It wasn't that I didn't drink. I'd been drinking since I was thirteen—three years, by this point. I just didn't drink with them. Now that Steve was drinking, I felt alone, even though he was in the next room. I wished he'd never taken a drink.

Our new apartment was dark and depressing and only had one bedroom. We'd been kicked out of the last place after Mom tossed the Christmas tree in the fireplace and almost burned down the house.

It was 1964, and I was a sophomore at Pasadena High. I skipped class all the time. I knew there wouldn't be any repercussions for me; Mom didn't care. Being in school only reminded me that I wasn't smart enough. And besides, I had a crush on a guy named Charlie and all I was interested in was finding a way to see him. I didn't know which of the three lunch periods he had, so I cut class to make all three.

When summer came around, a bunch of friends from school went to Costa Mesa, about fifty miles south of where we lived. Every family who could was renting an apartment on Shalimar Drive. Steve and I asked Mom if we could go and if our friend Grant could come with us. Mom was okay with it, and we found a furnished apartment to rent. Greg stayed behind to work that summer, but he loaned us his Vespa scooter. Steve drove me and Mom and all our stuff, Grant drove the Vespa, and the four of us headed out to Shalimar Drive.

Life was good on Shalimar Drive. Steve stayed at the apartment most days, drinking and listening to music on his stereo. Mom went to bars or stayed with boyfriends. And Grant and I rode Greg's Vespa to Newport Beach, spread out our beach towels, and laid out to get tan. And then I met Stephanie.

Stephanie was also a sophomore at Pasadena High, but we had never met. She had curly auburn hair and wore a headband to keep it off her face. Her almond-shaped eyes were light brown and she was blind in one of them from tuberculosis as an infant. And she had the funniest, most contagious laugh I'd ever heard. Stephanie and I talked for hours while we soaked up the sun.

Grant and Stephanie hit it off as fast as she and I had. We all hung out on the beach all day, listening to her entertaining stories about her family. She found the humor in it all, and we laughed with her until we cried. Stephanie thought Grant looked like the TV news anchor Grant Holcomb. By the end of the first day we spent together, Holcomb was Grant's new name.

Stephanie's family was on vacation in Newport Beach for a couple of weeks, and they dropped her off at the beach every day to hang out with her friends. When her vacation ended, we asked her parents if she could stay with us for the rest of the summer. They dropped Stephanie and her suitcase off at our place on Shalimar Drive, as clueless as she was about what she was getting into.

My mom was in trouble again. She'd been arrested for being drunk in public and was spending two weeks in the Orange County jail. I was nervous. What if my friends found out? Of course the first thing Stephanie did when she got to our place was ask about my mom. But my brother and I already had an excuse ready: Mom was with her sister in Los Angeles for a couple of days.

She was released from jail a couple of days later. She followed right away when we asked her how Aunt Ruth was.

"Oh, she's just fine," she said, smiling as she met Stephanie.

Stephanie flashed her big grin and put out a hand to shake my mother's. "Nice to meet you, Sue. Your nails sure are beautiful."

My mother seemed to like that, so she kept talking to her. We followed her to the bedroom, and she started to peel her clothes off to take a shower. On her underpants, in large print, were the words ORANGE COUNTY JAIL.

I looked at Stephanie. Stephanie looked at the underpants. And then she burst out laughing.

From that moment on, I knew I could tell Stephanie anything.

As the weeks went on, we fell into an easy routine. After a day at the beach, we'd wash our hair, set it with big rollers, hop on the Vespa, and drive around until our hair was dry. In the evenings there were parties on our block, and we'd see old friends and make new ones. I was always terrified that my mom would show up.

Mom's welfare check came on the first of the month, and she paid the rent and utilities and bought some food. Holcomb and Stephanie bought their own food, which made things easier. Everything was going fine—until the day we got an eviction notice. The landlord didn't think our water hose fights with the next-door neighbors were funny. So we packed up and moved to another apartment a block away, which turned out to be next door to some surfers we'd seen at school. These were the popular seniors from Pasadena High!

The day we moved, Stephanie and I were carrying the last boxes in from the car when a tall redheaded guy came over and introduced himself.

"I'm Bob," he said. "Can I give you a hand with anything?"

"Thanks, but this is the last of it," I said, setting down a heavy box. I wanted to get a good look at our new neighbor.

"I've seen you two on the beach at Fortieth Street," he said, running a hand through his hair.

"We've seen you too, Red," Stephanie laughed.

"Can't miss that great laugh of yours," he said. "Hey, my roommates and I are having a party on Saturday. Like to come?"

"We'd love to!" we chimed. After Bob left, we carried our boxes inside, closed the door, howled, and high-fived.

Living next door to the surfers from Fortieth Street was as much fun as we thought it would be. They had good parties, but there was one drawback—it was way too easy for my mom to crash them. She would walk in without knocking, ask for a beer, and then ask one of my friends for a ride to the bar.

Our last party of the summer was in the middle of nowhere, off the beaten path in the dunes and boulders. We had a huge bonfire, flaming torches, and buckets of beer. Couples were cuddling and making out, saying goodbye after long summer romances. Bob and I took a seat on a flat rock near the bonfire. He handed me a beer.

"I'm sure glad you moved next door. It's been great getting to know you," he said. He put his arm around my waist and pulled me close. "I hope you'll let me take you out after you get settled in your new apartment." We kissed and talked until only embers glowed in the fire pit.

* * *

We moved back to Pasadena when the summer was over, and Mom rented a two-bedroom apartment. Bob called only a week after we moved in and asked if I'd like to go to dinner. I couldn't wait. But I was nervous. Mom had been sober for a few days, but then she started talking about Gloria again, and before long she was drunk.

The night of our date, Bob looked different. Maybe it was the shirt and slacks instead of surf shorts. Maybe it was the realness of going out with him. But I liked it.

Dinner with Bob felt special, with our patio seats outside and a pretty view of the city. But it was hard for me to relax without a drink. I'd been drinking all summer, and this time, for the first time while hanging out with Bob, I wasn't. I was so nervous trying to make conversation. Thank God we could talk about memories of the summer and plans for school.

After dinner, he took me home, walked me to the door, invited me on another date, and kissed me goodnight.

School was a lot more fun now that I had a boyfriend and a best friend. I spent half of my junior year at Stephanie's house. I liked her family, they always had food, and I could get away from the depressing scene at home. Plus, she had a lot of clothes and always let me borrow them. Stephanie and I went everywhere together. I stayed at her place all week, and Bob and I spent the weekends together, going to dinners, movies, and parties.

Eventually, Bob and I fell in love. We would park in a spot overlooking the city or on a street near my house and make out. When he tried to touch my breasts, I would push his hand away. I knew from the talk around school that girls weren't supposed to have sex before marriage or they were considered cheap, easy, or sluts. I didn't want to be any of those things.

Bob and I continued our weekend dates and make-out sessions throughout my junior year and into my senior year of high school, and I could see his frustration mounting. I was tired of turning him down. I was turned on too, and I didn't like having to be the one to put a stop to going further.

Bob was a great guy and a wonderful boyfriend. One night, I finally let him touch my breasts. But I couldn't get out of my head! I kept thinking, *What's going to happen now? Am I really doing this?* And my thoughts were keeping me from relaxing, from being present, from being able to feel. It didn't do anything for me. I thought it was supposed to feel good! I figured there had to be something wrong with me. I couldn't let Bob know. It might hurt his feelings that his touch didn't do anything for me. I worried he would know there was something wrong with me and he wouldn't love me anymore. So I faked it. *Ooh* and *aah* went a long way. And Bob seemed to love it.

I decided to eventually let Bob touch me down there—another disappointment. I didn't get any pleasure, but I moaned as if I loved it.

Stephanie had a boyfriend now too—a surfer friend of Bob's named Bobby—and we often double-dated. Bobby had a woodie, the surfer's car, and once in a while they took us surfing with them. We'd load our boards into the back of Bobby's woodie and drive up and down the coast looking for good waves.

Stephanie and I told each other everything. Neither of us had "gone all the way" with our boyfriends. And we were both tired of disappointing them. One night at her house, we came up with a game plan.

"We'll lose our virginity," I said. "We just need the right place for it. We'll do it at the same time so we can compare notes!"

Right away, I knew the perfect place. Greg rented a two-bedroom house in Newport right on the beach. I called him and asked if the four of us could stay at his place sometime soon. He said it would be fine; he was going away the next month.

"But no parties," he warned.

I promised it would only be the four of us. I could barely sleep that night. I mean, really, how romantic could it get? Making love for the first time in a cozy little beach house? We'd hear the waves crashing, smell the salt air, wake to the sound of seagulls.

I was pretty nervous about actually doing it, but so was Stephanie. Would we like it? Would it hurt? Would they still respect us? Would the word get out that we were easy?

A few weeks later, the four of us were on our way. Stephanie and I knew our boyfriends carried condoms in their wallets just in case we ever said yes, but they had no idea of the surprise they were getting that night. Bob brought a bottle of wine from his parents' house. I was happy he did. Something to calm my nerves. We ate dinner at a nice restaurant, and then we went to Greg's beach house. We quickly chose our bedrooms, Stephanie gave me a wink, and we all disappeared behind closed doors. Everything went as planned—until the morning.

Our boyfriends were surfers, after all, and no matter how great the night was for them, they were on surfer time, which meant they were out of bed the second the sun touched the horizon. Bob woke me with a kiss on my cheek, whispered that he'd see me soon, and was gone. I opened my eyes to see the bedside clock: 6:00 a.m. I crawled out of bed to find Stephanie. As I glanced back at the bed, I noticed a reddish-brown spot on the sheet.

Sex was a mystery to me. There was no sex education in school. My mother never talked about it. I had seen her in bed with a boyfriend, but I'd never seen her having sex. Still, I knew what she was doing, especially when her bed was in the living room. She never acted like there was anything wrong with being naked in bed with a boyfriend, and I really didn't mind. What I minded was her drunkenness and

the fact that most of the time there was almost nothing in the house
to eat.

I flung open my door and ran smack into Stephanie on her way
to get me. We sat close on the living room couch. I heard the seagulls,
which made me feel a little sad. I'd dreamed of hearing that sound
while lying wrapped in Bob's arms, our bodies nestled in soft sheets.
And look at us. Our boyfriends weren't even there.

"Well," I said finally, "it kind of hurt. I didn't want him to know,
so I didn't say anything. Thank God it didn't last long."

"It hurt me too!" Stephanie said, pressing her knees together.

"I did a lot of *ooh*'s and *aah*'s," I said.

Stephanie nodded fast. "Yep, me too. Me too."

"And guess what," I whispered. "There's blood on my sheets."

"There's some on mine too!" Stephanie said, slapping her thigh.

"What a disappointment. Why is it such a big deal?" I asked.

"Who knows. But we better get our sheets washed before they
come back," Stephanie said.

We jumped up and headed to our bedrooms to strip the beds.
We walked to the Laundromat at a strip mall down the block, hugging our bundles tight. I could always count on Stephanie to find the
humor in anything, and she didn't fail me on this one. We laughed
all the way there.

It was getting close to graduation now, and I could hardly wait.
Mom wasn't drinking, which made it easier for me to have Bob
over. He was enrolled in Pasadena City College, and he and I did
our homework together while Mom played solitaire. Everything was
going great.

Then, one day in April, I was caught smoking in the bathroom.
Because I cut class so much, instead of being suspended for a few
days, I was expelled. Two months before graduation. I didn't want to

be a high school dropout. Deep down, I believed I was going to be a success at something; I just had no idea what that might be.

The building that held the continuation school looked like a house and was just as comfortable inside. I went to school on time every day and never cut class. I worked at my own pace, smoked cigarettes on breaks, and got to leave by 1:00 p.m. I loved my new school.

In June of 1966, I passed the GED and graduated in cap and gown at the Rose Bowl with the other seniors at Pasadena High. I only invited Bob. I didn't invite Mom or Steve, who were drinking a lot. I figured Greg had better things to do. It was easier for me this way.

Our entire graduating class celebrated Grad Nite at Disneyland. I thought it would be more fun if we drank, so I stuffed a few miniature bottles of rum in my bra. High school was over, and the rest of my life was about to begin.

Chapter Four
Work Experience

Not long after graduation, I opened the phone book and looked for the biggest ad there was for an employment agency.

Stephanie lent me a conservative navy-blue dress for my 9:00 a.m. appointment. I curled my hair, put on some makeup, and put on a new pair of stockings. At last, I could get a full-time job and have some money of my own. Even though I felt nervous about the whole thing, I needed a job, a good job. I felt uneasy, but I stuffed my feelings down and walked in anyway.

The receptionist handed me a clipboard with papers to fill out. Yikes. *Work experience?* I didn't want to write down my job serving food at Fedco. *Skills?* The checkboxes didn't apply to me. *Typing speed?* They had to be kidding. I handed the clipboard back to the receptionist and took a seat, my palms sweating.

I wondered what job they could offer me. Maybe I'd be a bank teller. I heard secretaries could have some pretty cushy jobs. All of the other women in the room thumbed through magazines while they waited for their names to be called. I chose a copy of *Cosmopolitan* and paged through it, wishing I had painted my fingernails like the other women had.

At 10:10, the receptionist finally called my name. We walked through a large room filled with desks, where women were either on the telephone, typing, or talking with other young hopefuls like me.

"How many words do you type?" she asked. I couldn't answer. I had no idea. She looked at me and batted her false eyelashes. "Per minute. How many words do you type per minute?" she asked again.

"Oh!" I laughed. "About thirty." That seemed like a good number.

"Do you use a Dictaphone?" she asked. My stomach plunged. "Do you use a Dictaphone?" she repeated, staring harder at me.

My heart pounded hard and my forehead broke into a sweat. Nausea flooded me. I couldn't speak. My tongue was frozen. Without looking up, I grabbed my purse and fled the room, ran down the four flights of stairs, and left the building. The street bustled with cars and people ready for the workday. I couldn't breathe; I was gasping. I paced the sidewalk, wanting out of this feeling. I took a deep breath and let it out with a big sigh.

This was my first panic attack. If only I were twenty-one, I could have stopped for a drink to calm down before I got there that morning. But I was only eighteen.

I called Stephanie and told her what happened. I told her how awful I felt, how I felt like I was being judged. She understood. She'd gotten a job as a credit checker at a bank downtown, and she said I should come down and see if there were any job openings.

I was there the next day, and the manager hired me on the spot. It didn't even matter how fast I typed. I called Bob right away with the news. He wasn't impressed. I always felt he'd be happier with a smart girl.

He thought I was wasting my time working as a credit checker. He thought I should go to City College, do something with my life, get some higher education. But I wasn't interested in college. If I had any plan at all, it was to fall in love, get married, and have children.

For the past year I had been thinking of how I would break up with Bob. We had been seeing each other for three years, and I was bored. There was nothing new to talk about, and I was so tired of sex in the back seat of his old Chevy.

Luck was with me: Bob graduated from college and moved a couple of hours north to Santa Barbara to continue his education. Now we could end our relationship because of the long distance! Neither of us shed a tear.

Once Bob was gone, I decided to enroll at Pasadena City College and take night classes that interested me: psychology, French, and social science. I didn't care if I graduated; I just wanted to see if I could get good grades when I paid attention. I was also single and ready to date. Maybe I would meet someone!

A few weeks into the first semester, I was getting good grades in social science and psychology. I liked these classes. I was actually learning, and I felt good about myself. Maybe I wasn't dumb after all. But French was hard. I was bored and restless during French.

One night in French class, I found myself thinking about how I'd had an especially bad day. Work was bad, I got stuck in traffic, and I didn't have time to grab dinner. And for what? Verb conjugations? I made my escape—I always sat in the back, so it was easy for me to slip out unnoticed.

I crossed the street and walked into a pool hall with a crowd inside, mostly guys. I loved the sound of pool balls striking each other. I bought a candy bar and a Coke. I wished I had a beer.

I walked around, scoping out tables, looking for one to drop my quarter onto to save my place for the next game. One table was being run by a cute guy with dark wavy hair and brown eyes. I liked his look. And he was a good player too, sinking one ball after another. I put my quarter on the edge of his table. He looked up with a smile.

"I'm David," he said, chalking his cue stick.

"My name's Patty," I told him. I chose a stick from the rack and faced him with a smile. "Let's go."

He turned to the table and broke the balls with a loud crack.

"First time here?" he asked.

"Yeah. I just skipped out on French class," I told him. I liked the way his hair fell across his forehead when he looked at me.

"You'd rather shoot pool," he said.

"Exactly," I said.

"Glad you came in," he said. I blushed.

I was a pretty good player, but I was no match for this guy. For the next few hours we flirted and shot pool. We talked about surfing. He had a blue nine-foot Dewey Weber. I told him that I surfed once in a while on my ten-foot Hobie. I hoped he was impressed. I think he was.

At the end of the night, David asked me on a date for Saturday night and I gave him my phone number. He drove me to my car in the school parking lot, and I drove home to call Stephanie. I didn't care what time it was.

On Saturday, David picked me up in his red Mini Cooper. He took me to dinner in Malibu, somewhere I'd never been with Bob. I liked that—everything was new and better. David was easy to talk to and more of a free spirit, like me. Bob was so serious.

After dinner, we took a walk on the beach and talked more. He was eighteen, just like me. He worked at In-N-Out Burger and shared an apartment with two other guys. He planned to go to college the next year to major in business. We sat on the beach and kissed until the sun disappeared.

At home later that night, I told Stephanie over the phone, "I'm worried he won't like me after he meets my family."

"Just tell him about them before he meets them," she advised. "Get it over with so you won't have to worry so much."

The next week, David took me to see a movie, and then we stopped for a burger.

"When you come over, don't be shocked by how things are at my house. My mom drinks a lot," I told him.

David shrugged. "It's fine. I don't care. And nothing could change how I feel about you, remember that."

On our next date, David picked me up and met my mom and Steve at the door. They were both drunk. Mom stood there, swaying.

"So you're taking my daughter out. What makes you qualified?" she slurred.

"I guess you'll have to ask Patty," David told them. "But we have to go. We have a dinner reservation at seven."

"You just got here!" she protested.

"We don't want to be late, Mom," I insisted.

"Who cares, they can wait. Where are you going?" Mom kept on.

"Bye, Mom. See ya, Steve!" I waved.

"Good to meet you both," David said, and we walked out the door.

＊ ＊ ＊

That summer, I was flying high. I had a new boyfriend who didn't mind my family, liked double-dating with Stephanie and Bobby, and partied with me every weekend.

We started having sex, and I liked the kissing and the passion, which was much more than I'd ever felt with Bob. It gave me hope, but I didn't think it would get much better. The sex wasn't very interesting. I reverted back to making sure he enjoyed it by faking it again, moaning and groaning. I thought if I didn't fake it, if it didn't seem like I liked it, no one would want to be with me. I couldn't just lie there like a dead fish. I thought I was broken.

One night, we were drinking at a party, and while we were dancing, David held me close and asked, "Will you marry me?" In shock and without thinking twice, I said yes, and David twirled me around to celebrate. But we were both so drunk that we lost our balance and I slipped, fell on the floor, and hurt my back.

He helped me to the car and drove me home. Even though I was in pain, I was excited about our engagement. "I'll check on you tomorrow," he said when he dropped me off. "We'll shop for a ring."

The next morning, Stephanie took me to the doctor. On the way there I told her about David asking me to marry him. "He was so drunk," I told her. "Maybe he doesn't remember." Deep down, I thought he would have changed his mind when he sobered up. How could anyone want to marry me? How could I ever be enough?

The doctor gave me pain pills and told me to stay in bed for two weeks. David called every day to check on me. But he never said another word about marriage.

My back healed, David and I dated for the next three years, and then, finally, things started to cool off between us. I couldn't seem to get the courage to break up with him, but yet again, fate intervened: David was drafted in the spring of 1969. Now I knew two people in the army: Greg had already been drafted and was in Vietnam.

* * *

With David gone, I started looking for a new job. I never liked my job at the bank, and Charlie, a friend from high school, said there might be an opening for a secretary position at the stock brokerage firm where he worked. I thought that maybe things were starting to look up—maybe I'd meet someone at Charlie's stock brokerage firm and we'd fall in love, get married, buy a big house, and have three beautiful children.

The next morning, I went to the brokerage office for my interview. A receptionist greeted me and led me through a huge room with a dozen desks divided into rows. The walls were glass from floor to ceiling with a breathtaking view of Pasadena nestled beneath the hills. This was the place. I belonged here.

I was introduced to a good-looking man with a baby face and blue eyes, Mr. Carson. He didn't look much older than me.

"Call me Ron," he said. "Everyone does."

He motioned for me to take a seat and went back to his oversize reclining swivel chair.

"I need someone right away," he said.

"I can start today, if you like," I suggested.

"That's wonderful," he said.

I thought, *What? No interview?*

"Charlie told me good things about you," he continued. "You're in."

He showed me to my new desk, just outside his door, and called everyone's attention.

"This is Patty, everyone. My new secretary," he announced.

Everyone looked up and waved and gave me a smile. He took me on an office tour, greeting everyone by name as we passed. In the mail room, he introduced me to my new assistant. I was twenty-one years old, and I was a secretary at a stock brokerage firm with my own assistant!

That first day, I typed a few letters, did some copying, and ran trips to the mail room. When I left at the end of the day, I found a pay phone and made a call to quit my job at the bank.

My new job was fabulous and the pay was great. I was earning enough to rent a three-bedroom, two-bath apartment with Stephanie and a couple of our friends, Karen and Sharon. The four of us got along fabulously. I felt good about myself. I was financially independent!

One evening, I got home from work and my stomach fell to the basement. My mom's beat-up suitcase was next to the front door. My roommates weren't home and Mom was nowhere in sight. I called Steve.

"She's probably staying at the Green Hotel with some guy," he said. "At least that's where she said she was staying when I saw her a couple of weeks ago."

I drove to all of my mom's regular bars looking for her. I'd done this so many times over the years when we needed money for food. She wasn't at any of them, not even 35er, her favorite bar. This time, I was really afraid of what she was up to. But she was nowhere to be found.

"I can't believe my mom did this. I'm so embarrassed," I told Stephanie.

"I like your mom," she reassured me. "She can sleep on the couch if she wants to, what the hey."

A leaden feeling was creeping over me, and I wanted it gone. "Let's drink and have some fun tonight," I suggested. "Want to go dancing?"

"I can't," she said. "Bobby and I are going to a movie."

"Sharon!" I shouted. "Want to go dancing?"

I heard Sharon shout, "Yes!" and she was in the doorway in seconds.

Sharon had a big crush on a guy who played in a band at a club called The Clinic. It was a hot summer night, and I wore my pink hot pants and white leather go-go boots. We ordered beer at the bar and checked out the crowd.

I noticed Josh Singleton, a popular guy from high school. My stomach flipped. I elbowed Sharon just as she whispered, "Josh Singleton is here." She smiled at me and urged a little too loud, "Go over there! Go say hello!"

Josh was handsome, with sun-streaked light brown hair he wore combed straight back. I didn't know Josh very well. I had talked to him only a few times at school and at parties. I downed my beer, threaded my way through the crowd, came up behind him, and gave him a tap on the shoulder.

"Patty!" He raised his beer. "How you doing?"

The band was so loud we had to practically yell as we caught up on each other's lives. After a couple of beers, we danced for a while, and then we sat down to catch our breath.

"My parents have a beach house in Ensenada," Josh said. "It's been empty all summer, and they want me to drive down next weekend to check on it. How would you like to go with me? I leave Saturday morning and get back Sunday night."

I couldn't believe it. Josh Singleton was inviting me to go away with him, and we hadn't even gone on a date. We'd never even kissed! This was perfect. Maybe this trip was just what I needed to escape my worry about my mom. I wrote my address on a matchbook cover. As Josh stood to leave, Sharon walked up to our table. Josh said hello to her and tucked the matchbook in his pocket.

"I'll pick you up at nine," he said.

When he disappeared into the crowd, Sharon looked at me with raised eyebrows. "He'll pick you up at nine?"

I smiled at her. "We're going to Mexico on Saturday."

Chapter Five
Buzzkill

"Do you know how we got into this room?" Josh asked, squinting. We woke up in our clothes on a still-made king-size bed in a hotel room as the sun glared through a huge window.

"The last thing I remember was ordering dessert," I said, staring at the ocean just outside our room.

The day before, Josh had picked me up in his yellow Porsche convertible at 9:00 a.m., and we'd driven with the top down all the way to Tijuana. Josh suggested we make a quick stop in Rosarito Beach, and in no time, we were drinking beer and shooting pool at the Rosarito Hotel. At some point, we decided to get tacos.

"With a shot of tequila for dessert!" I suggested. I always needed to keep drinking. Otherwise I believed I wouldn't be enough fun. I didn't want Josh to regret inviting me.

We got up and hopped back into the Porsche. Back on the road again, Josh drove us fifty miles to Ensenada. I reminded him I had to be back by six o'clock that night because I had work in the morning.

"We'll go right to my parents' house, make sure everything's okay, and head back," he assured me.

As soon as we pulled into Ensenada, I saw a sign for Hussong's Cantina.

"Did you know that's the one spot where everyone goes? It's famous!" I told him.

"Should we stop for a beer?" he asked.

"Yeah, just one!" I cheered.

"A beer" ended up being three pitchers and some shots of tequila, and by four thirty, we were back on the road. As we pulled up to Josh's parents' beach house, the drinks were hitting us hard.

"Hey," I said as we stepped inside, "do your parents have any beer in the house?"

"Let's see." Josh opened the fridge. "Yep. Plenty of beer."

I leaned against the counter to steady myself, and Josh came over and kissed me. Reality hit as the sun started to go down.

"What time is it?" I asked Josh.

"A little after six thirty."

"I should call my roommates," I said. "They'll worry about me."

I called, and Sharon answered the phone. I told her I was having a great time and wouldn't be back until about eleven o'clock. She told me not to hurry.

Somehow, within what felt like a few minutes, it was already nine thirty. This time I called my friend Charlie from work.

"Hi, Charlie," I said, trying to keep my voice as natural and clear as I could. "It's Patty. I'm in Mexico. I won't be back to work until Tuesday. Will you please let our adorable boss know?"

"Is something wrong?" Charlie asked.

"No. I'm just having way too much fun and Mexico is so far away, so I thought I'd stay a little longer. And Josh is really nice and we're going back to Hussong's in a while and you're such a good friend, Charlie."

"Patty," said Charlie. "You sound loaded. You better sober up and get to work by Tuesday because if you don't, you won't have a job.

Ron won't put up with this sort of thing, I can promise you. I recommended you because I thought you were responsible."

"Okay, okay, Charlie. I am responsible," I said. "I'll be there Tuesday. Bye-bye from Mexico!"

"What a buzzkill," I said to Josh as I took another tequila shot.

Deep down I knew I had to keep drinking; I wasn't ready to even think about how much I'd messed up or what the consequences would be.

That night, Josh and I had sex. Not because I wanted to; I didn't even like him that way. I'd known from the beginning I wasn't good enough for him. He was really popular, and I thought he was out of my league. But he was nice, and I thought he expected me to have sex with him. He did take me on this trip and all. Afterward, Josh passed out, but I grabbed the bottle of tequila and headed out to the beach.

I opened my eyes in the morning with a blazing hangover, not remembering how I'd gotten back. I told Josh I thought we should cool it with the drinking and start getting ready to drive home. I thought I could somehow make it to work tomorrow morning, and since it was Monday, I hoped the traffic wouldn't be so bad.

"It's Wednesday," Josh corrected me.

"Wednesday! Are you serious?" Had I been blacked out for two whole days?

I called Stephanie, and she sounded strange.

"It's not good," she said. "Charlie said you got fired."

"Okay," I said, feeling even more depressed.

Josh and I were quiet all the way home. All I could think about was how I'd let everyone down. Charlie had recommended me for this great job, and now he would never want to talk to me again. I screwed up so bad. How would I pay rent? Where could I get another job right away? Why was I drinking so much? I vowed never to drink again.

I got home at three o'clock on Wednesday afternoon. My roommates met me in the living room, and the tension was thick.

"We're not mad," said Stephanie. "But the rent is due in three weeks. And you just lost your job."

"I know. And I'm going to do everything I can to get another job right away," I assured them.

"Even if you get another job right away, I don't know how you're going to pay rent in three weeks," said Karen. "And we don't want to lose this apartment."

"We've already found another roommate," Sharon confessed. I couldn't believe it. I'd been fired only yesterday, and my roommates had already replaced me.

"One of the credit checkers is moving in," said Stephanie. She took a seat next to me and put her arms around me. "We feel bad too. If you get another job, you can move back in with us. It's going to be okay."

I couldn't even look up. I went to my room to pack my things and prepared myself to move back home.

* * *

Living with my mom and Steve was harder than ever. I found a part-time job at a sandwich shop and a part-time job at a donut shop. Neither job brought in enough money to move back in with my friends, but at least I was working.

One night, Stephanie called me, sobbing. I could barely understand her.

"Bobby crashed his car," she sobbed. "He died."

It was hard to believe. Everybody loved Bobby. He was such a big part of our lives, and now he was dead. Stephanie was devastated. Within weeks, she quit her job and moved to Las Vegas, where she became a blackjack dealer at the Las Vegas Hilton.

I hated that Stephanie had moved so far away. I felt alone without her. I missed the fun we had. I missed her great laugh. I was twenty-three years old and unmarried, and now my best friend was gone. Something big had to change in my life. Most of my high school friends were married, and Karen had just gotten engaged. What was wrong with me? I didn't want to be an old maid, and that was on its way to happening if I didn't find Mr. Right soon.

Not long after Stephanie moved, I answered an ad in the newspaper for a job at a food brokerage company in South Pasadena working in the mail room and on the switchboard. I was hired. It was a good job and the people were nice, but I was still unhappy. What was the life I wanted, and how in the world could I get it?

That summer, I suggested to Sharon that we take a break from work. We both called in sick to our jobs for a while and tried to get fired. It worked. We would collect unemployment and enjoy the summer off.

One day, we drove by a billboard while on the Pasadena Freeway that read:

LIVE WHERE THE FUN IS
APARTMENTS FOR RENT
YOUNG-ADULTS COMPLEX

By nightfall, we had rented a furnished one-bedroom with a small kitchen and a bar, all utilities paid. There was even a swimming pool.

That summer, we lay out by the pool during the day and danced at The Clinic at night. Bennies kept our weight down and our energy up, and our main diet was iced tea. There were lots of parties in our building. If we weren't out dancing, we were partying at home. Sharon was dating Nick, a singer, and I dated his brother, a drummer. But no one seemed to interest me for more than a couple of dates.

One sunny day, Sharon and I were sitting on our balcony when I saw a guy ride a big Harley down the steep driveway that led into our parking lot. He wore his dark hair in a ponytail and a T-shirt with cutoff sleeves that showed off his big, muscular arms. He looked great riding that bike. I thought to myself, *Now there's a guy who's in my league. I'd be good enough for him.*

"Sharon, do you see that guy?" I pointed. "I'm going to marry him one day!" The words just flew out of my mouth, and somehow I believed them.

A few days later, I saw the Harley guy again. I watched him talking to his friends; he had lots of them. I decided to walk to the pool when a guy stopped me to say hello.

"Patty! Remember me?" he said. He looked a little familiar, someone from the apartment parties.

But I couldn't take my eyes off the good-looking guy standing beside him—the Harley guy with the ponytail.

At last, Bert and I were introduced.

Chapter Six
The Harley Guy with the Ponytail

I had just hung up the phone with Steve when I heard a motorcycle roaring outside. I jumped up and peeked out the window. The sound of the engine grew louder. I stepped back so I couldn't be seen. And then the engine quit. I couldn't believe he was here. I was nervous. And excited.

"Hey, Pat!" Bert yelled. "You home?"

I threw open the front door and grinned. He was sitting on his bike, his hair tight in a ponytail, a red bandana across his forehead. "Thought I'd stop by. What are you up to?" he asked.

"Staying home for a change," I flirted. He smiled and looked at me curiously.

"Do you smoke weed?" he asked. Weed? No one had ever offered me weed before.

And there it came, out of my mouth before I knew what I was saying: "Yes," I lied.

Bert stepped inside and took a seat on the couch, looking handsome as he held a joint up to his face.

"Light it up!" I said, hoping I sounded cool.

He tapped the seat beside him. "You're too far away."

My stomach fluttered as I took a seat next to him. I watched him take a puff and then pass it to me. I took a small hit and handed it back. I was so relieved to not feel any different.

He finished the rest of the joint, and we talked for a couple of hours. He told me he worked as a machinist at Lockheed Aircraft. Before that, he'd done three years in the army and served one of those years in Vietnam. He had been married briefly, had a child, and was divorced. He saw his daughter, Stella, on the weekends. He was the eldest of five brothers and had one younger sister. He grew up in the projects in East Los Angeles. He was a good dancer in high school.

"I've really enjoyed tonight, but I've done most of the talking," he said. "I'd like to take you out and get to know you better.".

And then he kissed me. His kiss didn't turn me on; it was just okay. But everything else about him did.

Bert called every day after that and took me to dinner at least three times a week. About a month later, we were at my apartment making out on the living room floor when he suggested we move into the bedroom. I didn't say yes, but I didn't say no, so he took my hand and led me to my bed.

My jaw dropped the minute I saw him naked.

"They called me Horse Dick in the army," he said with pride.

In all of thirty minutes or so, Bert had a great time. Still no pleasure for me.

I didn't expect sexual pleasure. Not even from a horse dick. Not that I knew what sexual pleasure was. I didn't even wonder. I was just happy that he liked me. I told Bert, Stephanie, and Sharon that the sex was the best ever. And at that time in my life, it was.

No one could understand why a girl like me was with a tough guy like Bert. Sure, he was maybe a know-it-all and a bit argumentative, but who wouldn't need a little armor growing up in the projects? I didn't care. He was good to me. Things were going along just fine.

But one day, I took my car in for service. I was working at a local car-rental agency, and Bert showed up at my office at closing time to offer me a ride since it was raining. I told him I would just follow him to my house in a rental car.

It was pouring. The visibility was terrible. I followed Bert's taillights through the city and onto a freeway on-ramp. I gripped the steering wheel, trying to keep my breathing even, but my heart was pounding hard. I could honk my horn to get his attention, but would he know it was me? Would he know what I meant? What I meant was I didn't want to do this!

I followed Bert's taillights right onto that freeway anyway. The windshield wipers slashed at the rain, but they were useless. I gasped for air as my chest tightened and my heart raced. Where was an exit? What would Bert think of me if I didn't follow him? I didn't care anymore.

I took the next exit I saw. I pulled over and turned off the engine. I had never had a panic attack while driving. I wanted a drink, anything to calm me down. I started up the car and drove as slowly as I dared until I found a supermarket. I bought a six-pack and sat in the car and drank a beer straight down. Right away, I started to relax enough to drive the rest of the way home.

Bert was there when I pulled into the driveway, so I quickly grabbed some mints from my purse; I didn't want him to think I was an alcoholic. He was worried about me and thought I might have been in an accident. I told him that I'd had a panic attack and needed to pull over. He agreed it had been a rough ride, it was a hard rain, and I was in a car I didn't know. We hugged and sat on the couch, and Bert lit a joint while I opened a beer.

Monday morning, I left for work as usual, got on the freeway, and had the same horrible reaction all over again. What was wrong with me? I hated feeling out of control like this. I got off at the first exit and took the city streets the rest of the way to work.

* * *

Six months passed, and Bert and I were in love. We had been talking about getting an apartment together, and one on the other side of the parking lot became available. It had a big living room and a picture window with a view. We decided it was time.

We moved in, and I decorated. It looked spectacular—until Bert brought his motorcycle into the living room. As someone dedicated to making our home beautiful, the sight of that motorcycle in our living room drove me nuts. But I never said a word. Bert loved that bike, and I didn't want to cause a rift between us by saying something.

I was thrilled the day Bert had his bike up and running and out of the living room.

"Would you like a ride on the back?" he asked me.

"Sure, sounds like fun!" I lied.

I didn't let on that I was absolutely terrified as we rode on the freeway in and out of traffic in the freezing-cold night. It was horrible for me, but I wanted to be whatever I thought Bert wanted me to be. Even if that was a biker chick.

It wasn't long before we started talking about getting married and buying a house. I designed my engagement ring and our wedding bands, and we had them made. They were beautiful and we loved them.

Bert didn't get down on one knee, but I was fine with it; we already had lived together for two years and we talked about getting married all the time. He just put the engagement ring on my finger, and it was official—we were engaged.

Bert was eligible for a VA mortgage, so we were able to buy a beautiful home with a pool in LA. We got two adorable puppies that we played with all the time, but I wanted to be a mother more than anything in the world, and I wanted to be married first.

Two years passed, and we set our wedding date for June 2, 1973. I was twenty-five. We saved enough money to do it in style and have a Las Vegas wedding—just us and four of our closest friends. I didn't even consider inviting my mom and Steve, and Greg lived in Hawaii, which seemed like too far to travel. Stephanie was my maid of honor, and for me, that made everything perfect.

Once Bert and I were married, things changed right away. Bert sold his motorcycle. I stopped taking birth control pills; I couldn't wait to get pregnant. I even cut back my drinking to only one glass of wine in the evenings. I knew it wouldn't take long; we had sex every day. Bert had a strong sex drive, and because I faked pleasure so much he probably thought I wanted even more sex than we were having. Sometimes we had sex twice a day.

In June of 1975, our first child was born, a son we named Bert. We found it confusing to have two Berts in one house, so I started calling our baby Popeye because he was bald and had large forearms. The nickname stuck. At last, a child to love and care for, someone I could nurture the way I wanted. Pure bliss. I was filled with more love than I had ever felt in my life. I loved bathing him, breastfeeding him, rocking him in my arms until he fell asleep. I felt honored to be his mother, blessed and fortunate to be the one responsible for him. I couldn't understand why Bert wasn't as enchanted with parenting as I was.

He would watch a football game while holding Popeye, and I'd think he wasn't appreciating him enough.

"You're wasting him," I'd say. "Give him back to me. I won't waste him."

Maybe deep down I feared our baby could be neglected like I had been. One thing I knew for sure was that our son would never be neglected by me.

I wanted everyone to see Popeye, including my mom and Steve. I took Popeye over to their house early one morning, knowing it was the only time they would be sober. They were, but my mom didn't look good at all. Her skin was sallow, and she looked worse than the last time I'd seen her. Neither of them reached out to hold Popeye or tug at his little collar like people usually did. They looked at us with discomfort, like they didn't know what to do with us. Despite their reaction, I continued to visit them every once in a while, but it always felt awkward.

Before long, I was pregnant again, and in December of 1976 I gave birth to our beautiful daughter, Dawn. A daughter! I held her to my heart and promised her I would be the best mother in the world to her and that we would be close, able to talk about everything. I cherished every minute with her, holding her and looking into precious, innocent eyes that looked back at me with complete adoration.

* * *

A year later, I returned to the same hospital, only this time it wasn't about birth. My mom was dying.

In June of 1977, I left the kids with Bert and drove my mom to the hospital with Steve. She was so sick that she didn't even know my name. She kept calling me Susie, and I didn't even know a Susie. I called Greg with the news, and he flew in from Hawaii.

My mom was put in intensive care for a few days and then put on life support. Stephanie flew out to say goodbye, and she cried as she did. I watched her saying goodbye to my mom and felt very sad, but there were no tears in me.

At only sixty-six years old, my mother was dying from cirrhosis. Mom couldn't get sober. And I couldn't cry for her. It felt almost like a stranger was dying. It broke my heart to know she would never get to watch her grandchildren grow up.

We all knew Mom wouldn't want to be hooked up to a machine, and knowing that made it easier to give our permission to turn off life support. Steve was very close to her, and it was probably the hardest for him. He cried as I put my arms around him, and I offered comfort with the same words he had said to me so many times when I was very young: "It'll be all right, Steve; it'll be all right."

Within a few days, our mom was transferred to intensive care at Huntington Hospital in Pasadena, the hospital where my children were born. She was unconscious and cold. Only a sheet covered her, and I asked the nurses to put a blanket over her.

"At this point, a blanket isn't going to warm her up," a nurse told me.

A wave of sadness washed over me as I sat at the foot of the bed holding my mother's icy feet and trying to make them warm. I told her how sorry I was that she'd had such a hard life. I told her I was sorry that Gloria was killed, that she had to live with so much pain, and that she couldn't stop drinking. I told her I loved her very much.

Just as I was ready to leave, Steve arrived, and he followed the nurses as they took Mom upstairs to a private room. He was at her side when she died in the middle of the night.

It wasn't unexpected, but it wasn't the sorrowful moment I thought it should have been. When the doctor told me and Greg the next morning that our mom had passed away, we just looked at each other and had no words.

Chapter Seven
The Last Time

I knew Steve would take our mom's death especially hard, but I had no idea what an impact it would have on me.

Bert had never approved of my mom, so I never felt like I had permission to cry. But one day, when I was alone in the kitchen, it finally happened. I cried. The grief poured out of me, grief buried so deep that I had no idea it was inside me. I was mourning that my children would never get to know their grandmother. I was mourning that I never got to know my own mom.

I called Steve, and he was drunk and crying so hard that I couldn't make out what he was saying. I hated that he was alone now. I decided to visit him.

When I got to his apartment, he wasn't home. I spoke to his neighbors, and they told me he was pounding the booze more than ever. One night, he'd even gone berserk and thrown the TV set out the window.

Now that my mom was gone, her Social Security checks stopped coming, and Steve became homeless with his dog. I felt terrible, but even so, I didn't invite him to live with us because he drank so much.

On numerous occasions he tried to quit, sometimes staying sober for up to a month, but the detox was so severe that he always ended up drinking again. I tried to support him with positive thoughts and told him I was sure he could do it. "Don't give up, Steve!" I'd tell him over and over again.

I started attending Al-Anon meetings while Steve panhandled and slept in a sleeping bag behind a Laundromat in San Gabriel. Every once in a while, I would visit him at a nearby park and bring a picnic for us to share. Our relationship would continue like this for years, and even under these circumstances, I was happy to have him in my life. It did both of our hearts good.

* * *

Four years later, when I was thirty-one years old, my son Rocky was born, another wonderful blessing with adoring eyes. It felt so good to have another son; two boys and a girl was just what I'd always wanted. When I held Rocky to my heart, I could feel how special he was. Now our family was complete.

Every day I woke up amazed at my good life. I had been married for seven years, had three children, didn't have to work, and could spend all of my time with my children. There was nothing on this earth more important to me than being a good mom. Laughing and playing with them, giving them big hugs, and telling them how much I loved them was the highlight of each day. I even found time to sew the cutest clothes for them. In the evenings after I put them to bed, I'd have a class or two of wine—I felt so fulfilled buy them that I didn't feel the need to drink any more than that.

Bert's job at Lockheed Aircraft was going well. He was a hard worker, always taking any overtime he could get. He even had a side job once in a while and still took time off with our family for summer vacations. Bert gave us everything we could want. We lived in a gorgeous home, I drove a new car, the kids went to private school, and I never had to worry about money. When Bert came home from work, the house was clean, a delicious dinner was cooked, and we ate together as a family. I was the perfect wife and the perfect mom.

Bert's daughter, Stella, had stayed with us on the weekends since she was three. She was thirteen now, very sweet, and was great with her younger brothers and sister. Popeye was almost seven, Dawn was five, and Rocky was two. I embraced Stella like my own.

One evening, Bert came home from work and said he wanted me to go to a party in Beverly Hills with him. Dan, a big-shot lawyer, was hosting, and he wanted Bert to come over and build a gym for his house. I figured it couldn't hurt for Bert to earn a few more bucks, but we didn't go out much anymore, and rarely without the kids.

"Come on, Pat," Bert urged. "All you do is mom stuff."

Stella agreed to babysit. I put on a pretty cocktail dress and heels, and off we went in our shiny burgundy Cadillac. It was hard leaving the kids. I missed them already. Unless we were talking about the kids, we didn't have much to talk about. But I told Bert I'd do my best to have a good time.

At the party, I was introduced to Dan and his wife, Debbie. We hit it off immediately. And there was a mariachi band performing on the staircase! Debbie had flown them in from Mexico City as a surprise for Dan. The house was alive with music as people sipped cocktails and nibbled appetizers. I linked arms with Bert and followed him outside to the patio where people were lined up at a table.

"What do you think they're doing?" I asked Bert.

"Dan's giving them hits of cocaine," he said. "Wanna try it?"

Cocaine? Not me. I'd heard about people getting hooked on that stuff. I hung back as I watched Bert snort a line from a mirrored platter. Still sniffling and dabbing at his nose, he took his place next to me and squeezed me around my waist.

"How is it?" I asked, checking his eyes.

"Mmm," he hummed. "I haven't felt this good in a long time. You should try it."

Maybe he was right. It looked harmless. I got in line and copied what everyone else did. The buzz was immediate.

"Wow!" I said to Bert, feeling a brightness flow through my veins, a good feeling I'd never felt before. All night, I talked with everyone, completely free and uncaring, until I looked at my watch: 3:00 a.m.

"Bert!" I screamed. I told him what time it was, and we were out of there in minutes.

I was relieved to see the kids were asleep like little angels in their beds. Bert had already tumbled into bed and was fast asleep, but I was wide awake.

At 6:00 a.m., I whispered the words out loud: "I will never take cocaine again."

It was Bert's responsibility to go to work and pay the bills and my responsibility to take care of the kids and the house. I loved it that way, and I wasn't going to do anything to ruin it.

Two weeks later, Bert asked me to go with him to another party at Dan's. I agreed, sure that if anyone offered me cocaine, I would turn it down. Even if Bert didn't.

That night, a group of us went into Debbie's big walk-in closet to admire her gorgeous clothes. Then, out of nowhere, she offered us some coke. Of course. I'd already had a couple of drinks and didn't feel as concerned about it anymore. So when the others said they'd love to, I was right in line. One by one, we inhaled a line, thanking her when we were through.

I excused myself to find Bert, annoyed with myself for giving in so easily. This was definitely the last time. I found Bert on a couch in the living room, and I cuddled up next to him. In only a few minutes, someone handed us the mirrored platter. I didn't even comment. Bert went first, and then it was my turn again.

On our way home, Bert said he was going to make some extra money selling coke for Dan. He assured me things would be all right, that he would be careful. I was used to him growing and selling marijuana for extra money, so it didn't come as a big surprise that he wanted to sell coke. And I wanted all the things the extra money could buy.

Before long, Bert was using cocaine on a daily basis. Not long after that, Bert told me he had been laid off from his job. He hadn't been punching in on time for quite a while. My stomach dropped.

"Take it easy," he assured me. "I can do more work for Dan. We'll be fine."

Around this time, I started drinking more—and I started drinking earlier in the day, which was another thing I'd never waned to do. But it helped calm my nerves from the coke and from not getting enough sleep. I had wanted Bert to drink more too so he wouldn't do so much coke, but that had backfired. Now he was drinking and doing more coke than ever.

Break dancing was popular at the time, and Bert started practicing it on a dance floor he made on our patio. At night he would practice Michael Jackson's moonwalk until 4:00 a.m. It was impossible for me to sleep with all the racket—thank God the kids' rooms were on the other side of the house and they never heard him. When he was finished dancing, he would come in and wake me up for sex. I pretended I couldn't wake up, but it didn't matter. He kept trying, pestering me until he knew I had to be awake. I couldn't refuse him. I just lay there and thought to myself, *This is the last time I'm going to let him do this to me. The last time!*

It got even worse when Bert started to get paranoid. He thought the police were going to arrest him at any moment, and his anxiety was through the roof. One night, he grabbed my hand and pulled me outside.

"Look up," he said. "See those dots, Pat? You think those are stars? They're not. They're FBI cameras. They're taking pictures."

He had a telescope set up in the living room to aim at the cops he thought were hiding in the bushes surrounding our house. If I told him there were no cops in the bushes, he got angry at me for hours and told me over and over again how I needed to be aware of everything around me.

"They're everywhere," he'd say. "Everywhere."

Before long, everything seemed to be about using and selling. I told Bert I wanted a normal life again. He wasn't eating dinner with the family anymore. If I wanted to go to a movie or dinner with him and the kids, he didn't care.

"I'm too busy," he'd say. "We'll do that when things calm down."

When were things going to calm down? Bert was so caught up in his work and his all-nighters that nothing seemed to have an effect on him. Maybe if I got mad and yelled a little, it would get his attention. But I was afraid that I'd go too far, and I wasn't ready to find out what that would be.

One night while the kids were sleeping, I moved out of our bedroom and onto the couch. Six months passed with me sleeping on the couch, and Bert wasn't fazed by it. I pretended I was asleep while he walked around the house, pointing his gun out the window toward the bushes. I was so glad the kids were sound sleepers and never saw him when he was paranoid like this.

I started trying to tell him that I wanted a divorce. But he never took me seriously, because every time I said it, I was drunk. Drinking was the only way out I knew. Drinking was the only way I had the guts to tell him I was unhappy. I was a mess. I'd be drunk and frustrated that things weren't getting better, and I would inevitably end up doing coke. And every single time, I hated the outcome.

One day, Stephanie called. She told me I had been calling her almost every night at 3:00 a.m.

"Patty," she said, "do you know that you're an alcoholic? I'll come out and watch your kids if you'll go to rehab."

I was crying as I said yes and accepted her offer. I was angry. Angry at myself for doing coke in the first place. Angry at myself because I'd let my kids down. Angry because I was doing exactly what I promised myself I would never do. Angry at Bert for not being willing to quit. Angry because I was an alcoholic. Angry because I was sick and tired of needing alcohol just to feel normal. Angry because I was repeating the pattern my mother had started so long ago.

Stephanie and I made plans for her to come, but once I realized she would arrive in a couple of days, the reality set in. The thought of being away from my children for three weeks tore at me. Drunk, scared, angry, and depressed, I decided to drink and do more coke than ever.

When Stephanie arrived, I was a complete mess. I yelled at her, blaming her for wanting to put me in a hospital.

"I can't believe you," she said. "Fine then. I'm out of here."

"Oh, no, you don't!" I shouted. I started hitting her. I had never hit anyone in my life, and now I was hitting my best girlfriend for trying to help me. Bert came in at the sound of all this commotion, saw me out of control, and, without a word, slugged me in the jaw.

"Stephanie," I said, letting her help me up. "Get me out of here. Take me to the hospital."

But if I was going to quit, this was going be my last hurrah.

"There's never enough!" I shouted as I grabbed a bottle of wine to drink on the way. "Stop at my friend's house. She has some pills."

Alone I lay at St. Luke's Hospital, feeling sick to my stomach, aching with pain, so deeply sad. I started private and group counseling, and every day I felt a little better. My children visited on Sundays.

"You don't seem sick," Dawn once said.

"That means I must be getting better," I told her.

This was exactly what my mother had said to us so many years ago. I couldn't believe I was here. Bert was sure I was being brainwashed, and one day he came to the hospital with a gun in his briefcase. He demanded they let me go, the staff called security, and the guards walked him off the grounds. They assured him he would be arrested if he ever did it again. I sat on my bed, hugging my knees, wishing I could be free of him.

Every counselor came in for an intervention with me, urging me not to go back home with my husband. They wanted me to go into another rehab facility for six months.

No way. I missed my children. I had already been away for twenty-one days. I promised I would never drink alcohol or use coke again. I would be a good mom. And if Bert didn't stop the drugs and alcohol, I would get a divorce. Whatever it took, things were going to change.

Chapter Eight
Nothing Could Be Worse

Fresh out of rehab, at dinner with Bert, it was strange not ordering a drink. But I was glad to not even want one, even though I was nervous about going home. I asked Bert how he was doing. Was he drinking? Was he using coke? He told me he'd quit both.

"I'm great," he assured me. I didn't like the sound of that. I didn't believe things could be different. I'd only been gone for twenty-one days.

As we ate in silence, I wondered if I could stay in this marriage, if I could resist drinking and be a better mother to my children. I was thankful for Antabuse, a pill I would take every day for six months. If I had a drink on the pill, I would get violently sick and be back in the hospital.

Back home, I opened the front door, and the kids ran into my open arms, laughing and squealing with joy. Everyone talked at once, telling me what they did while I was away.

That night, I did my best to step right in. I helped the kids with their homework. I made sure they practiced their musical instruments, took baths, and had everything ready for school. When they were all tucked into bed, Bert asked me to come to our bedroom.

"What do you think?" he said, gesturing toward a beautiful new brass bed. He wanted me to give him another chance to prove he had changed. Bert didn't have wine at dinner, and he didn't seem high. If I was given a chance to be a better mother, I wanted to give Bert a chance to be better too.

The next day, I made calls to Stephanie, my sister-in-law Rita, and Bert's mother. I wanted to let them know how much I appreciated them helping out while I was away. I thanked Stella for being such a wonderful big sister to the kids. Everyone was happy to hear me sound so good.

I did the laundry, cleaned the house, and went grocery shopping while the kids were at school. But being home again wasn't as easy as I thought it would be. When the kids got home, it seemed like they all wanted my attention at once. Had they always had this much energy? It was a lot for me after the quiet of my hospital room.

I'd changed in the hospital. In fact, I'd changed more than I realized. When Bert shouted from the other side of the house, "Pat! Coffee!" it felt different. When he did it before, I always felt disrespected but never complained. Now I pretended not to hear him. I didn't know how to tell him I didn't like being spoken to that way.

Just like I didn't know how to tell him I didn't like his nickname for me: Bitch. I always used to take it because my standards were already so low and I had no boundaries because I didn't feel good about myself. He didn't mean it in a negative way, but I wished he called me something nice, like "honey" or "sweetheart." The best I could do was call him Bozo. He laughed the first time I used it—he had an Afro, after all—so I took that as permission to keep calling him that.

It seemed like Bert was telling me the truth about quitting drinking and using coke. He was attentive, waiting on me hand and foot. In fact, he was overattentive, and it started to get on my nerves.

"Do you need anything? Do you want a sweater? Do you want me to get you something to eat?" he'd insist.

I was beginning to get suspicious. But by my fourth day back, I didn't have to wonder anymore. He started break-dancing again. For hours. When I accused him of using, he begged me to believe he wasn't. And then I walked in on him doing it.

"It's all I have, really! I just wanted to get rid of it," he swore.

"Nothing has changed, Bert!" I shouted. "I'm out of here! I'm sleeping on the couch!"

I stormed out, disappointed and angry but also impressed with myself. I'd spoken up while I was sober!

For the next three months, Bert went out to the backyard to break-dance. It was obvious things weren't going to change. I'd had enough.

I stopped taking Antabuse. I was drunk when I told Bert I wanted a divorce, and I was drunk every time I repeated it. I told him I wanted him to move out, but he refused. I was done pretending I was asleep on the couch while he walked around all night pointing his gun out the window. I was done with his break dancing. I was done with his paranoia. I was done with his lies. I was done with the entire lifestyle.

One day, Bert finally said the words I'd been waiting to hear: "Okay, I'll go." I watched him grab his jacket, get in his car, and drive down the street. I was thrilled. I envisioned a normal life, just me and the kids. There would be no drugs, and I would stop drinking. What a huge relief.

Then, minutes later, I heard Bert's car come back up the driveway. He threw open the front door and barged in, fuming.

"I've changed my mind, bitch. If anybody's leaving, it's gonna be you and the kids. You've got exactly three minutes, or I'll blow you all away!" he shouted.

Terrified and trembling, I moved as fast as I could, running through the house to grab my purse and car keys and gather the kids. We got in the car and I drove away, promising myself I would never come back, no matter what. Nothing could be worse than living like this.

I had fifty dollars in my wallet and no checkbook with me, not even my Sears card. Rita and her husband, Jim, lived nearby, and they let us stay with their family for a couple of days until I could figure out what to do.

My heart broke when I put the kids to bed that night. We missed Stella already, as she'd stayed with her dad. And it was Dawn's eighth birthday. I felt terrible for Dawn; what a horrible birthday. I promised her we would celebrate that weekend, that we'd all go out, but I had no idea what I could do with no money.

I took off my wedding ring and thought about "until death do us part." There was a death all right, a death of well-being for everyone in the family. The next day, I found a pawn shop and traded it for some cash.

After a few days with Rita and Jim, Bert's brother, Matthew, and his wife, Shelly, said we could stay with them for a few days. From there, we moved to Shelly's sister's house for a couple of weeks. Being homeless was getting old really fast. I had to do something. I asked Matthew for a loan of a thousand dollars. It was hard to ask for money, especially because I couldn't say when I'd be able to return it. But he was happy to help. Bert's siblings knew how difficult Bert had become, even if they didn't know the half of it.

I rented a small two-bedroom house, got a phone, and had the lights and gas turned on. We still didn't have any clothes or furniture, but I was able to get beds and blankets from the Salvation Army. I had to get the kids into school—since we'd been on the move, I didn't know where we'd end up and what schools they would eventually attend, and now we lived in a different district. They had already missed three weeks, so after we moved in, I got the three of them enrolled right away.

Meanwhile, Bert was going ballistic. Somehow he found out that Matthew had loaned me money, and he threatened to kill him or anyone who tried to help me. He put a lock and chain on the gates in front of the house so I couldn't get any of our things. He was using so much cocaine and was so paranoid that it was impossible to predict what he would do next. I wasn't about to expose the kids to him or try to explain any of it to them. It was painful.

The kids hated leaving their home and friends, especially with no warning, no chance to say goodbye, no chance to pack their things, no chance to get used to the idea of moving, no chance to say good-bye to their dad. They had no idea their parents' marriage was in trouble or that their father had become dangerous because of drugs. I told them every day that things would be better soon, that I felt horrible they had to go through this. I swore to myself we would move to a nice neighborhood and that they would have everything they were used to having.

Soon there was no money left. We were able to receive welfare and food stamps, but it wasn't enough. Because Bert and I owned our home, a lawyer was helping me pro bono to file for divorce and custody and apply for child support, but that would take a while. It was time for me to get a job. While the kids were in school, I cleaned a woman's house for six dollars an hour—twenty-four dollars a day. It was a good start but not nearly enough to live on. The shadow of my own childhood was dark and looming.

While looking for a second job, my car broke down. It was a big Cadillac, and repairs were expensive. With smoke coming out of the engine, I pulled into the nearest gas station, where the owner told me it would cost three hundred dollars to repair.

"I don't have that kind of money," I told him. "Could I leave my car here while I figure something out?"

"I can help you," he said, smiling. "I can take it in trade."

I was so shocked by his words that I wanted him to explain himself, in case I was making the wrong assumption. He looked older than me, with thin receding hair combed back from his face.

"Make me happy for an hour," he said.

"I don't do things like that," I told him. "I'll be back with the money to pay for it."

He reached into his shirt pocket for a business card and pressed it into my hand.

"In case you change your mind," he said.

I assured him I wouldn't be calling.

For the next few days, I thought of everything I could. It made no sense to even try to get more hours housecleaning now that I was stuck without a car. I barely had enough money to buy food, and the kids needed more clothes and shoes. I needed clothes too. The rent was coming up again in two weeks. I couldn't lose our house. The stress got to me more and more and I was drinking more and more, which was exactly what I swore I wouldn't do.

On the third sleepless night, I started thinking about the man at the gas station. Maybe I could do it. I could have my car back, I could buy food, and I'd have two weeks to get the money together for next month's rent.

The next morning, I poured myself a glass of wine. My hand shook as I dialed the number.

"I'm only doing this because I have no other way," I told him.

Chapter Nine
Real Estate

I walked seven blocks to the gas station.

I got into the gas station owner's car and we drove to a motel nearby. The ride was torture. The odor of grease from his soiled clothes was overwhelming. I talked out of nervousness—about the weather, the beautiful trees this time of year. He talked about his children, pointing out their school on the way. He seemed so relaxed that I had the feeling he had done this before, probably many times. But he was my first, and he would be my only. I couldn't wait until it was over and I could forget it ever happened.

To my relief, it was over in ten minutes. By the time he put on the condom and got close to me, he was done.

On the ride back to the gas station, I kept thinking how lucky I was. The fear of it had been much worse than the real thing. Now I could get my car back and find a second job.

Two days later, the phone rang. It was him again. He'd told his cousin about me.

"I'm doing just fine," I assured him. "I don't need that kind of help."

But then the week passed without any job offers, and I drank more to ease the pain. What was I going to do? I decided I could do it just once more, to get enough money to pay the rent on time.

I drove myself to the same motel. The gas station owner's cousin and I went to the room. He told me about his job and family troubles. "I hope things get better for you," I told him, genuinely.

Again, my stomach churned. I pulled down a familiar curtain over my heart and acted like I thought a woman was supposed to act—like I was having a good time, like he was pleasing me. I figured if he was paying for a service, it was part of my job. When he was through, we got dressed, and he handed me sixty dollars. I had no idea what to ask for and assumed this was the going rate.

Back in my car, I had to smile. It wasn't as scary as I thought it would be. He was a regular guy, not drunk, not on drugs. And I'd just made more money in half an hour than I'd ever thought I could.

While the job hunt continued, I worked with the lawyer to finalize my divorce. Because I wanted custody, we had to go to court. Bert didn't show up for the first two court dates, and on the third court date, he walked into the room looking worn and sullen. He avoided my eyes, mumbled, looked away, and wouldn't give a prompt answer to any question he was asked. The judge granted me full custody of our three children and determined how much Bert would pay in child support. Oh, how I loved the sound of that gavel banging down: it was done.

The kids were all mine, thank God, but money was my biggest worry—I didn't get any money from the divorce because we had no equity in the house. And it was no surprise to me when Bert didn't pay the child support the court ordered. I went to the district attorney and signed papers so that they could garnish Bert's wages, but I never received a penny. So when the gas station owner's cousin called one day and asked to see me again, I said yes. Sixty bucks was sixty bucks, and I had to put food on the table.

In the next few days, I received calls from some of the cousin's friends. I pulled down that curtain over my heart and said yes every time. I continued to drink, though I was trying to drink less. I didn't want my kids to see their mother drinking all day, so I would get a Diet Coke from the convenience store in a big plastic cup with a straw, empty out the Diet Coke, and fill it with beer. I thought that this way, the kids wouldn't know I was drinking—even though when I was a kid, I always knew when my mom was drinking, whether I saw her doing it or not.

Throughout the day I sipped it slowly, just enough to stay a little numb and ward off a debilitating panic attack. I'd take my plastic beer-filled "gulpy" everywhere—to the grocery store, to Little League games, to the motel.

One day, I decided enough was enough. I was sick of living without my things and without my kids' clothes and toys. But I was terrified of Bert. I hired a private investigator to watch the house and find out when Bert wasn't home. It turned out that Bert was moving. The investigator said he would call me as soon as Bert left with his moving truck.

When the call came, the kids and I drove to the house, and our own moving truck followed behind. The gates were chained with a big padlock. One of the movers went to the back of his truck and pulled out a bolt cutter.

"Hurry!" I shouted. "Hurry, hurry!"

While the movers moved the piano, the kids' beds, the washer and dryer, and the TV, the kids and I were in the kitchen throwing dishes and pots and pans into boxes. My heart was pounding. I just wanted to get the hell out of there.

We were in and out of the house in an hour. The kids jumped into the car, and I climbed in and put my key into the ignition. But the battery was dead. I got out of the car and screamed at the movers, who were about to drive away. They jump-started my car. Thank God. My knees shook as we drove away.

As soon as we were out of the neighborhood, a smile came across my face. I did it. I imagined Bert driving up to the house all coked up and seeing the chains cut. He would run inside to see it was me who had been there, that I was the one who had cut the chains and taken back our things. It was me.

* * *

I wasn't drinking much when I first started the housekeeping job, and I was good at my work. But it wasn't long before I started drinking more, staying up late, and going to work hungover. I just wasn't motivated to work for six dollars an hour now that I had earned so much more. About a year after I started housekeeping, I was late a few times, and that was enough for them. I was fired.

Now that I had no other job, it was time to consider the alternative. I could see men for money a few times a week and make much more than I did as a housekeeper. As long as I didn't call it prostitution, I could handle it. It didn't seem like prostitution. I felt like I was the girl next door, earning a little extra money whenever I got a call; I wasn't soliciting work. I always thought of prostitutes as streetwalkers wearing miniskirts and boots. They were on drugs, forced to work by a pimp. That wasn't me at all.

I looked at all the benefits. I couldn't see any negatives. I could work short hours in the daytime, make decent money, and still have plenty of time to be home with my kids and go to their Little League games. It was really a pretty easy decision for me—I didn't feel bad about myself for doing it. It just made sense.

The gas station owner would sometimes give my number to his friends, and before long, I had my regulars. The money started coming in. There was no job security, but so far it was working. I never knew how many calls I would get in a month, or if I'd get any calls at all. All I knew for sure was that I had to hustle.

Before this, I'd taken the kids everywhere with me. Things were different now. I wasn't the available mom I had been all those years. It was so hard to say no when I was leaving to meet a client and the kids would ask, "Mommy, can I come with you?" They were curious. I had to make up a really good story about what I was doing every time I got a call. What could I be doing that didn't take very long? The motel was five minutes from our house, and I was home within an hour.

Then it hit me: I could say I was a real estate broker. But wait; I didn't know a thing about real estate. What if I was something like a real estate broker, a person who helped show houses? My boss hired me because he didn't have time to show all the houses himself; there were too many people who shopped without buying. The lie was perfect. I even came up with a name for my job: I was a real estate hostess.

I knew I had to just keep moving forward for now, supporting my kids with this work while hoping that someday I would be able to find a way out of it. So I bought a pager. I kept it on me all the time and returned calls in private. It was the only number I gave out. Now everything was going to be fine. Because I was a real estate hostess.

* * *

Our house was one of six small houses sitting close together on a single lot. All of our neighbors were nice. Sam, the man who lived across from us with his eighteen-year-old son, spent a lot of time in his garage and always said hello when we passed. Sometimes he and I would chat. Sam was a nice-looking man with dark brown hair and eyes. He was a simple man, not too complicated. He had worked at a tool and die shop for twelve years. I liked how much he loved his son.

Before long, I was making excuses to go outside in hopes that Sam would be in his garage. One day, he told me that he went to the golf course for breakfast in the coffee shop on Sundays. He invited me to join him the next week. I was going on a date!

In no time, Sam and I were officially dating. In the evenings on his way home from work, Sam would pick up a fifth of rum and call me to come over and share it with him. It was easy to go home and check on the kids, just forty steps away. It may have been just forty steps, but it may as well have been forty miles, considering the kind of mother I had become.

Most nights I would put the kids to bed by eight o'clock, even in the summer, while it was still light out. I would sit and drink with Sam, paying more attention to him than my own kids. This became a routine, and my kids were suffering just like I had, when I was their age and Victor showed up.

One morning, I got up and found a note from Popeye that read, *MOM— I HATE YOU.*

I threw the note away, then took another drink to numb the pain. My worst fears had come true. I had become a horrible mother.

I had become *my* mother.

Chapter Ten
For a Good Time

"I had no choice," I said quietly.

"I get that," Bert said. "I've just never seen that side of you before."

A few months had passed, and Bert had called. He apologized for the way things had gone. And he was glad we'd gotten our stuff back, even if it meant doing it the way we did.

"After what I've been through, I'm not the same. I'm stronger," I said.

"I can see that," he replied. "Good for you."

He wanted to see the kids. I couldn't see why he shouldn't see them, since I'd heard from the family that he'd stopped using coke and wasn't drinking much. And I knew the kids missed him. I told him he could see them, but I wanted him to wait out front for them rather than come to the door. I wanted it clear that my house had boundaries he needed to respect, that *I* had boundaries.

Every couple of weeks for the next few months, Bert picked up the kids and took them out for a few hours. It went smoothly; he honored my terms and never walked up to the door. About two months in, though, he started calling and asking to see me too. I refused. But he persisted.

"We don't have to get back together, Pat. I just want you to come over for a little while," he pleaded. "I miss you and I'm horny."

I wasn't interested. At all. But there was one thing I wished I could get back from him—my favorite painting, the one that had hung on our dining room wall. It was a still life of a copper pot, colander, and vegetables. It was already gone when we went to the house with the moving van that day.

One night, I was pretty rummed up and feeling sad that Bert had taken it. That painting felt like home, and I wanted the kids to feel the feeling of home. I called him.

"If you give me the painting," I told him, "I'll see you for an hour."

"Really?" he asked.

"An hour," I repeated. "And I go home with the painting."

The next day, I arrived at Bert's apartment at exactly 10:00 a.m.

"Hello," I said, very businesslike. "Where's the bedroom?"

Bert raised his eyebrows and led me through a modest living room, where I saw the painting hanging on the wall. We entered his bedroom, where the king-size bed with the shiny brass headboard waited.

"Shall we get started?" I suggested, unbuttoning my coat.

"So what's all this?" he asked, unbuttoning his shirt. "You always walk around like this now?"

Underneath my coat was my champagne satin-and-lace teddy. I ignored his comment. I wanted him to feel my lack of care for him. And I made sure not to do one bit of faking pleasure. I kept checking my watch. At precisely eleven o'clock, I stood up and reached for my coat.

"Time's up, Bert," I said. "Gotta go."

I took the painting right off the wall. He was speechless.

Home with my painting, I started thinking about what else I could get for trade. Men seemed willing to barter for something that wasn't hard for me to give. I was used to turning out; I was good at it. And now, I wanted a large mirror for the living room, and I knew exactly where to get it.

The second I walked through the door of the downtown glass shop, I saw it. It was beveled, with a gold frame. I motioned for the shopkeeper. I told him my story about having all my furniture taken from me in a divorce and that I was trying to make a home for my three children.

"The walls are bare," I told him, "and this mirror would make it feel more like home."

"Mirrors can do that," the man said, reaching for a look at the price tag. I shook my head.

"You don't have to show me that," I told him. "I know what it costs, and I don't have the money."

He looked at me, and I held his gaze. Was I suggesting something? I was, and I let him know with the slightest of nods. He glanced again at the price tag.

"If you can stick around for a while, I can run the mirror up to your place and hang it for you," he said. I reached out for his hand to shake it.

I spent twenty minutes with him in a large office in the back. Afterward, we chatted and found out we had gone to the same high school and knew some of the same people. He'd been just a grade below me. He told me about some of his struggles since graduation; I offered compassion. We left in our cars, and he hung the mirror at my house.

"If your kids ever hit a ball through your window, be sure to give me a call. I'll be glad to fix it for you," he said before leaving.

I decided to try it again. I wanted to give my kids a Christmas like the ones they'd had before. I walked into a bicycle shop, and the same thing happened, only this time I got three bicycles for my kids.

* * *

The evening after I received the bicycles, I called Stephanie to check in on her. The last time we'd talked, she'd said the migraines she'd often suffered from were getting even worse and that the doctors couldn't figure out how to relieve her pain. A friend of hers, a nurse, told her heroin was the only drug strong enough.

"I'm hooked on it now," she told me. "I use it every day."

"Let's get you into rehab, Stephanie," I said. "You know it can help."

"No way," she said. "I'm not having those migraines again."

"Stephanie," I pleaded. "You helped me. Let me help you."

"No way, Patty," she said firmly. "I'm not going."

I wished Stephanie had never moved so far away. I hung up feeling worse than I had in a long time.

* * *

I'd been on my own with the kids for about a year and a half, and money was still tight. I wanted more for my children, with summer coming and the kids wanting to go out more with their friends. I just wasn't earning enough on a call or two a day. I dreamed of giving the kids a four-bedroom house with a swimming pool, the kind we had when they were born. Now the boys shared a bedroom, and Dawn and I shared the other one.

The kids were at school the day my brother Steve appeared at my door without warning. He was with a woman he introduced as his wife, Evelyn. She was a heavyset woman with long brown hair that looked like it hadn't been brushed. Steve looked better than I'd seen him look in a long time, and his voice sounded strong and clear. It was so good to see him.

There was beer in the refrigerator, but I didn't offer them one. I wanted to see how my brother was. Was he sober? I was just happy to see him again, looking as good as he did. We hugged each other tight, he assured me he was fine now, and we spent the rest of the day catching up.

That night, after they left, I thought about what I'd told Steve about Sam. I told him I'd been seeing him for about six months and that it was starting to get serious, which was true—Sam had become the most important man in my life. Maybe it was time to tell Sam the truth about what I did for a living. But how could a man accept that his girlfriend was a prostitute?

Later that week, Sam came home with the usual fifth of rum. I told him the whole story. He punched the wall with his fist.

"I knew I needed to tell you as soon as I knew we were falling in love," I assured him. "If I'd told you when we were first together, you wouldn't have gotten to know me. You know that."

He stopped pacing.

"Besides," I said, "I just told you my secret. I haven't told anyone else. I'm only telling you now because I'm falling in love with you."

Sam came closer and looked me in the eyes.

"I'm falling in love with you too," he said.

"It's my job, nothing more. It's about the money, not the sex. I always use protection," I pleaded.

He went to the front door and opened it wide, gesturing for me to exit.

"I'll call you tomorrow," he said. "We can see where we go from here."

The next day, Sam came home in good spirits. He invited me over and poured us a drink and told me his feelings about me weren't going to change.

"I know it's hard to raise three kids on your own. I understand how it started, and I get why you're doing it," he said. His expression was soft as he pulled me close. "We'll get married someday," he added, "but for now, we'll rent a big house with enough room for all of us under one roof."

We agreed to share the rent and split the bills, and I made it clear that I would continue with my work. Sam was okay with it, though I could tell that he hoped things would be different someday.

We found a big five-bedroom house in a good neighborhood with the best schools. It had a huge front yard with fruit trees, a swimming pool, and a pool house. It even had a badminton court. But the rent was expensive. How could I get more business? Now I knew I'd really have to hustle.

I went to a print shop and got business cards made. They read, FOR A GOOD TIME, CALL PATTY.

My pager number was on them, and that was it. Since my business had started with a car repair, I decided to start with repair shops. Every weekday morning for a few months, I got up early and handed out cards to mechanics. And most evenings, at least one call came in.

Now that I had more business, I was making much better money and could afford to live in this great house and to pay my half of the rent. And it felt so good to finally be able to pay back my brother-in-law the thousand dollars I'd borrowed from him.

The downside was that Sam was not easy to live with. He complained about the kids leaving their bikes in the driveway and problems with his son. The complaints were constant, and he wasn't fun anymore, nothing like he'd been when we first started seeing each other. After three and a half years together, I was tired of it. Sam and I ended our romantic relationship and decided on a friendship that would allow us to continue to live under the same roof, for the time being.

Right around this same time, Steve called. He and his wife needed a place to live. I invited them to move in with us and share the rent, and Sam was okay with it. They could stay in the huge living room we hardly used. They moved in right away. Now I could save the money to move.

Trouble was, now I had another drinking buddy.

Chapter Eleven
Nice Enough

I'd decided I would never date a client. Never. No client had ever asked me out, but I knew that if they did, I wouldn't agree to go. After things ended with Sam, I didn't want to be involved with anyone who knew what I did for a living.

So when Ted asked me out country-western dancing, my intuition told me to say no, but then I thought, *What the heck. I love country music, and he seems nice enough.* Ted was the manager of a local tire store, and for about six months, he'd been a client who I saw twice a week.

Ted and I ended up dating for six months, and then he surprised me with a marriage proposal. I made it clear that prostitution was the only kind of work I did and that I would continue to do it, and he understood. I loved Ted, but I wasn't in love with him, not in the way I wanted to be with a man I married. I hoped I would be able to fall in love with him, that something would eventually spark. So I agreed to marry Ted. It was 1989, and I would be a forty-one-year-old bride.

We had a small wedding in Ted's mother's backyard with cowboy hats, hay bales, and stacks of coiled rope. I put flowers on my cowboy hat and wore a denim skirt, white blouse, and my favorite pair of cowboy boots. Fourteen-year-old Popeye walked me down the aisle, Dawn was the flower girl, and Rocky was the ring bearer. Cold beers tasted especially good on that hot summer day, and from the time the wedding started to the time we left for our Las Vegas honeymoon, I was feeling no pain.

After our honeymoon, we found a three-bedroom house in San Gabriel to move into. It wasn't a big house, but I was thrilled to be moving away from Sam. And Steve and Evelyn would be moving out too—they had found a nice little duplex in Monrovia. It would be a good start for me, a new chance for a happy family.

As I was packing for the move, Ted called.

"You're not going to believe this," he said, laughing. "We left for our honeymoon without signing the papers."

Without signed papers, our marriage wasn't legal. But as soon as I hung up, I wondered if it was actually a good thing that the papers weren't signed. Maybe we'd overlooked them because this marriage wasn't supposed to happen. The truth was, I really didn't know this guy very well. We hadn't even lived together. As I continued packing, I hoped there weren't going to be any big surprises. But sure enough, there were.

Ted was possessive. He hated it when my pager beeped. He never said a word, but he would glance at me, scowling. If he was reading the newspaper when it beeped, he would turn the pages fast and hard. When I left the house, he'd say, "Have a good time," in a dreary voice, slowly drawing out each word. That drove me nuts. Months earlier, he'd told me he was fine with my work. He'd assured me over and over again that he would have absolutely no problem with me continuing to see clients. He'd promised. But I'd been hesitant. My intuition had told me marriage wasn't a good idea. But I still didn't listen.

Now that we were ostensibly married, it was clear Ted had a problem with me being a prostitute. I tried to reassure him that it was my job, nothing more. I showed him more affection in hopes that he would stop behaving the way he was. I wanted to give our relationship a chance.

* * *

About six months after the wedding, when I heard about a huge two-story house for rent in Arcadia, I took a look at it, and Ted and I decided to rent it. We took the master bedroom, and I was thrilled that the kids each had their own bedrooms again. Many of their friends lived in the neighborhood and came by often. I loved seeing them happy. The kids liked Ted. He took Popeye to his first concert and barbecued every week.

I wished Ted and I could be happy, but things weren't getting any better. I needed to work, but Ted reacted every single time my pager beeped. He was driving me crazy, and it was ruining our relationship. Eventually, I stopped trying to reassure him and I gave up on the hopes of ever falling in love with him. In fact, I started to resent him. I copped an attitude and found ways to drive him crazy too. Sometimes when I was drunk, I'd threaten to go out dancing without him—just like my mom would do to Victor. It drove him crazy every time. I was glad I'd never signed the marriage license.

* * *

About three years into our "marriage," Ted and I were watching a movie on TV, and the phone rang. I answered it.

"Can I speak with Ted?" said a woman's voice I didn't recognize. "Just tell him it's the cop."

The cop. It was his ex-girlfriend, the bossy one he'd left before we'd met. How had she gotten our number?

"It's the cop," I said, handing Ted the phone. Ted's eyes widened.

"The cop," he whispered.

I nodded. "The cop."

Cautiously, he put the receiver to his ear.

"Hello? Uh-huh. Okay. Yeah," he said, and he hung up.

"Why did she call here?" I asked, knowing that whatever he told me wouldn't be the truth.

"She called me last week. She was having a hard time with her daughter and wanted my advice," he said.

"Why didn't you tell me she called you? Have you been talking to her all these years?" I asked.

Ted always told me everything that went on in his day. Or so I'd thought.

"I didn't tell you because I didn't want you to think there was something going on," he said.

"If you had told me right away, I wouldn't have thought anything was going on," I told him. "Now I do."

I stormed into the bathroom and tried to collect my thoughts. I remembered how Ted used to call me at least five times a day just to say hello, to tell me what was happening at work, to say he loved me. Sometimes he even called to tell me what he had for lunch. And he always came straight home after work.

Ted is having an affair right in front of me, I thought. I could handle this. Then I thought, *Maybe he isn't. Maybe they are just talking things out.* I came out of the bathroom, apologized, and somehow got past it.

* * *

Ted had a ten-year-old daughter, Tori, from his previous marriage, and she was coming to visit—Ted hadn't seen her in three years. We'd been "married" four years at this point, and the kids and I had never met Tori; when Ted did visit her, he went on his own. Tori's visit would start with a barbecue at the beach with all of the kids. It would be a chance for all of us to get to know each other.

On the day of the visit, Ted was supposed to come home early from work to give us all more time together. When he was fifteen minutes late, I phoned his shop. The man who answered told me that he hadn't been there since nine o'clock that morning.

Tori arrived right on time, at noon. I told her that her dad was late and that I was sorry he wasn't there to greet her. Two hours passed without a word from Ted, and Tori and I sat awkwardly in front of the TV, channel surfing. I couldn't focus on anything but the clock. Finally, at two thirty, Ted's car pulled into the driveway. I jumped at the sound, and Tori followed me out front.

"Sorry I'm late," Ted said casually, as if nothing special was happening. "How are you, sweetheart?" he asked, reaching out to give Tori a hug.

"What's your story?" I asked.

"I had to go to the doctor to get my knee looked at. It was hurting again," he said.

"And you didn't call home?" I snapped. "I want your doctor's phone number."

"I don't have it on me," he replied.

"Then give me his name. I'll look it up," I told him.

Ted gave me his name, and I marched inside. I called the doctor's office while I watched Ted pacing in the driveway through the window. The receptionist told me she hadn't seen Ted that day.

When I reported this to Ted, he pleaded, "That's because I didn't actually see the doctor. A nurse looked at my knee because I didn't have an appointment."

"I'll just call again." I shrugged. Ted went back to pacing while I made the call. The receptionist confirmed that he had not come in that day. I went back outside to confront him.

"Look," I said, tapping him with a pointed finger on his chest. "I don't like lying. Your daughter, who you haven't seen in three years, is here, and this is not the time for us to go into this. But it isn't over."

The tension was thick all the way to the beach. I was furious. It was four o'clock, and there was no way I was going to set up a lunch after everything that had happened.

"You kids go with Ted," I told them. "I'm staying in the car."

"You can't stay in the car," said Ted. "If you won't come with us, we're going home."

"Then let's go home," I shot back.

As much as I wanted the kids to have a good time, I just couldn't go through with it. The kids shut the doors, and Ted took off. We drove in complete silence while I planned my next step. It was over between us, but I had to be careful. I didn't want Ted spilling my secret to the kids. He was emotionally immature and could easily threaten to do that. How would I end this relationship when he had so much on me?

At home I announced I was going for a walk. The kids were scared and wanted to come with me. Even Tori came along. We were almost at the corner when I noticed Ted's car coming up the street. I told the kids to duck behind some bushes. The kids seemed to think it was fun, which was a relief. We circled the block and finally snuck back to my car, and I told them to get in so we could go get something to eat.

At Maria's Cantina, I apologized to the kids. They ordered enchiladas; I ordered a double rum and coke. I told them that after dinner, we would go to a motel for the night, and Tori said she wanted to come too. But before the check came, Ted walked into the restaurant. My stomach flipped. He had been driving around, checking every restaurant parking lot in the area. To keep from causing a scene, I told him what he wanted to hear.

"I needed a walk, they needed some food, and we're ready to go home," I said as I motioned for the waitress.

"We can talk when we get back to the house," he said. "I'll pick up the check."

"See you at the house," I said as Ted paid and left the restaurant. "Okay, kids. It's time for an adventure!"

I drove us out of town, seething inside but hiding it from the kids. I wasn't going to let Ted ruin everything. We returned the next morning. I asked the kids for some privacy while I talked with Ted, who had been awake all night, worried sick. I told him I would need some time to forgive him and that he needed to leave me alone so I could get through this. I suggested counseling because I wanted him to believe I was actually planning to work through this, and he surprised me by arranging for an appointment right away. I agreed to go.

In the therapist's office the next day, he admitted that he'd lied about going to the doctor. This time his story was that he went to a friend's house to buy some pot. The therapist nodded, but I thought to myself, *Is she buying this? Because I'm sure not!* I figured he'd been with the cop all along. But it didn't even matter that I didn't believe him; I didn't care anymore. I'd already made up my mind about leaving.

Later that day, I told the kids Ted had been lying to me and that I couldn't continue my relationship with him. I said I was looking for a new place for us and that I wasn't going to tell Ted because I wanted peace in the house. The kids were on board.

Within a few days, I found a decent apartment on the other side of town, a two-bedroom with a big swimming pool. Instead of paying rent at the old place, I decided to use the money to rent this apartment on the spot and planned the move for the following weekend, while Ted was at work. All week, the kids and I packed everything we could fit into boxes and stacked them in the garage. Each night I sat on the living room couch with my packing checklist tucked under the seat cushion. Ted got down on his knees one night and told me how sorry he was. He begged me to come back and sleep with him in the bedroom. I told him to leave me alone.

On moving day, I would have seven hours while Ted was at work. The only thing I was leaving him was the king-size bed and the big TV in our bedroom, which were his to begin with. The rest of the furniture was already mine. My plan was to put a Styrofoam ice chest where the refrigerator had been and to fill the chest with ice and a few bottles of Dr Pepper. I thought he might be thirsty after he discovered the empty house.

As soon as Ted drove up the street on the morning of the big day, no one missed a beat and my plan went into full swing. I was nervous but relieved to be leaving, knowing that the kids wouldn't find out my secret.

Chapter Twelve
Madame Queen

Our new apartment was on a quiet tree-lined street, and it was heaven. Ted had no idea where we were. It felt like freedom.

But it was too small for an adult and three teenagers. The boys shared one room, and Dawn and I shared the other. The kids' friends were over all the time, and they raised a ruckus just like I'm sure I did that summer I lived near the beach.

On the plus side, now that they were teenagers, I could go out at night and leave them at home alone. On Friday nights, I started going to a karaoke bar called The Last Race.

The best karaoke singers from all over competed for a cash prize, and my favorite singer was a guy everyone called Matt Sinatra. Matt had the looks, and he was the most popular performer in the house. Everyone went wild when he won, which was often.

One night after Matt collected his winnings, he sat down beside me at the bar.

"What are you drinking?" he asked me. "I'm buying a round."

We talked and laughed for hours. Matt was tall, with sandy blond hair and piercing dark eyes. He looked a bit older than me, and I decided to ignore his white loafers. He was a golf instructor, after all. Besides, I liked how he looked with a double scotch in his hand.

I didn't mind that he could barely stand up at 9:00 p.m. I knew what it was like.

By 2:00 a.m., the bar was getting ready to close, and Matt and I were gazing drunkenly into each other's eyes. Somehow he got my phone number as we staggered to our cars, and somehow I got home safely.

A week later, Matt picked me up and we went to a dinner house called Dino's. Everyone was dressed to the hilt, and everyone seemed to know Matt. We had dinner, we danced, and then Matt Sinatra kissed me on the cheek and walked onstage.

He sang a few Sinatra love songs and even dedicated one to me. *Now this guy knows how to make a woman feel special*, I thought. I needed it after what happened with Ted.

Matt and I had sex once, went on a few more dates, and then one night he got down on one knee and held out an antique bracelet.

"I love you, Patty," he said. "Will you marry me?"

He loved me? He wanted to marry me? We'd only known each other for a month, and this was the first time Matt had ever said he loved me, but that wasn't the only problem. I was sure I didn't love him. But it felt good to be wanted. So I said yes.

Matt apologized for giving me a bracelet instead of a ring. The bracelet was his grandmother's, and it meant a lot to him.

"Oh, it's fine," I lied. "It's the thought that counts." All I could think about was how we weren't even in love. I wasn't about to let what happened with Ted happen again. Matt kissed me good night, and we drove home to our separate houses.

He didn't call the next day. Or the day after that. Three days passed without a call. I looked at the bracelet and thought, *How sad*. I barely knew the guy. I didn't even like him that much. I liked his singing.

That weekend, there was a knock at the door. There stood Matt, in his white loafers. Beside him stood two young girls he introduced as his daughters, Cindy and Kate. He'd never told me he had children.

"I have to give a golf lesson at one o'clock," he told me. "I have the girls today. Will you look after them for me? I told them you have a swimming pool, and they brought their suits."

I didn't want to make a scene in front of his daughters, so I politely agreed to watch them for a few hours.

But Matt didn't show up after a few hours. I was furious.

At 8:00 p.m., Matt showed up at the door with a story about losing track of time. There wasn't an apology, not even a thank-you. I put on my best fake smile and ushered the three of them out the door.

I was pissed. I was engaged to a drunk with the nerve to show up with daughters I didn't know he had, and now I was the babysitter while he went out to get drunk.

I never for even one minute wanted to be engaged to Matt. I just wanted to be wanted. I was humiliated that I'd even said yes. It felt degrading; I felt so sad that I was so desperate. I took off the bracelet. It wasn't even an antique; it was just old. I drove to Dino's, walked up to Matt at the bar, tapped him on the shoulder, and handed him the bracelet. He didn't say a word; he just took it and kept drinking. I never saw him again.

* * *

When June rolled around and the kids were getting ready for summer, I decided it was time for something new for me too. My work was steady—I'd managed to secure a number of regular clients—so money wasn't as tight as it had been. I was forty-five years old, and I wanted a boyfriend, someone to have a good time with, someone who would treat me well. I had six months if I was going to get a good start on a new relationship by the time the Christmas lights were up.

I thought of a place I hadn't been to in years: the North Woods Inn Restaurant and Bar, only two miles from home. The North Woods was a big, cozy place, a comfortable log cabin lodge filled with round tables and leather chairs, oil paintings, and Tiffany lamps. Bowls of peanuts were kept filled on every table, and ragtime music kept the place lively all day. I grabbed my cowboy hat and headed out. My plan was to take a seat at the bar, have a few beers, and scope out the place for any potential bachelors.

I got to the North Woods at 3:00 p.m. so I had time to warm up for the evening. I approached the bar and acted like I was looking for someone.

"Just a beer," I told the bartender. "I'm waiting for a girlfriend." I didn't want to look like a pickup.

I drank my beer and looked around. It was empty except for two men and a woman at the other end of the bar. The older of the two men had graying hair and a receding hairline, and his smile was warm and friendly. He caught my eye and waved a hand, inviting me to join them.

"No, thanks," I said. "I'm waiting for a friend."

"Join us till your friend shows up," he tried. He tapped the empty barstool on his left. What did I have to lose? I headed over.

"I'm Michael," said the man, extending his hand. "Nice hat."

The woman was his daughter, Ellen, and the younger man was their friend, Joe. Maybe Joe was the eligible bachelor I was going to meet! But for now, Michael had all of my attention with his news: they were celebrating his new stretch limo.

"Go on," said Michael, nudging me with an elbow. "Take a look at the limo with them. Joe, why don't you show them around?"

I followed Joe and our waiter out to the parking lot, and there it was: a platinum-and-white stretch limo.

I thought Joe was a nice guy, but I did like that limo, and it belonged to Michael. I liked that Joe was clean-shaven and looked trim in his black jeans. He was a little shy, which made him even more attractive. But I liked Michael too. Michael had a bit of a paunch, but his shoulders were wide and he looked solid and ready for a good laugh. His eyes were startlingly pale blue, and they had a kind of tired twinkle. He reminded me of Marlon Brando in *The Godfather*, only softer. And he was generous. Back inside, full glasses of beer waited in front of our seats at the bar.

"Get a good look?" asked Michael.

I nodded. "You know everyone here," I said.

"Been here every day since the joint opened thirty years ago," he replied. "Your friend hasn't shown up, has she?"

I was having such a good time that I forgot to act disappointed that my girlfriend hadn't shown up.

Ellen left, so now it was just the three of us. And the beers kept coming.

I liked Michael's style—smooth, confident, authoritative, friendly. He was out to have a good time, and so was I. Joe might have been better looking and closer to my age, but Michael had charisma.

Michael asked where I worked. I didn't miss a beat. "I'm in real estate," I said.

He hit the table with his fist. "So listen, we're going to a pre–Fourth of July bash tonight. Why don't you come with us?"

It was getting dark when we climbed into his limo and got comfortable on the soft burgundy seats. The limo's bar was stunning, lit with gorgeous crystal and filled with glasses etched with Michael's initials, M. C. Michael took a seat beside me, and Joe handed us each a cold beer.

"Listen, Joe's going to drive and I'm going to ride up front with him," Michael said. "You stay back here and have the place all to yourself. You will be Madame Queen."

Madame Queen, I thought. I liked the sound of it. I chugged my beer.

The party was in the Hollywood Hills, at a mansion bigger than I'd ever seen. We milled around, greeting people on the veranda. The view of the city was breathtaking and the buffet was spectacular, but I had no appetite. By now I was drunk and I found myself sitting on Michael's lap, and then on Joe's lap, not sure whose date I was. Maybe they were both my dates?

After the party, I found myself in Michael's kitchen at his house in San Gabriel, about two miles from mine, and he and Joe and I continued to drink. Michael put on some music and we all danced, and then we started kissing, and I do mean *we*. Michael and I kissed, and then Joe and I kissed. I wasn't sure how to turn things around, as drunk as I was, so I let it continue. They unbuttoned my blouse, and then off went their clothes and off went mine.

Michael pressed me close. "Why don't we each spend a little time with you in the bedroom?"

I wasn't thrilled by the idea—in fact, I really didn't want to—but I agreed. It was the first time in my life I'd ever done anything like this.

The next thing I knew, Joe and I were in the guest bedroom making out. In minutes, Michael came storming in.

"That's enough!" he shouted. "Everyone out!" He tossed our clothes into the room and slammed the door.

Joe started putting his clothes back on. "We better get the hell out of here," said Joe.

"What's wrong with Michael?" I asked, following his lead.

"He told me earlier he wanted you to himself," he said. "I know that's why he's pissed off."

We came out of the bedroom, and Michael was nowhere to be found.

By the time we got to Joe's, it was 4:00 a.m.

The next morning—or afternoon—we woke up, and Joe called Michael to apologize. I felt so ashamed. What the hell was I doing? I could have done better, but nobody had taught me how to have self-respect. And on top of all that, I hadn't been at home when my kids woke up that morning.

When Michael didn't pick up, Joe knew he was at the North Woods.

"He goes there every day at eleven thirty," he said. "Clockwork."

I headed home, and a few days later, Michael surprised me with a phone call. He asked me to lunch the next day at the North Woods, no questions asked.

The next day, we met in front of the North Woods at 11:30 a.m. We took a seat, and Michael set his briefcase on the table.

"Welcome to my office," he said.

"I've never seen an office like this before," I said.

"I do my work here. Keep up on the market, stay on top of my banking. It's hard work being retired, you know." He smiled.

He opened the briefcase and took out a copy of the *Wall Street Journal*, a silver Cross pen, and a writing pad. Then he took out a small flashlight and a battery-operated fan and set them on the table.

"You watch. If someone starts smoking nearby, I just blow the smoke in the other direction," he explained. The flashlight was so he could see the bill he'd sign at the end of the day.

Michael didn't want to hear about the other night. When I started to say something about it, he interrupted with a raised hand.

"We don't have to discuss that," he said. "My friendship with Joe is over."

I was shocked.

"I'm not sorry. I'd much rather spend my time with you. And besides, I'm tired of paying his way," he said.

My pager buzzed suddenly, and I checked it. "I've gotta go," I said. "But I'll be back in forty-five minutes."

Michael took a good long look at me in my tight jeans, tight T-shirt, cowboy hat, and cowboy boots. "Pretty snazzy outfit for a real estate agent," he said.

"I'm not an agent. I show houses *for* agents. They're the ones who can't wear their cowboy hats. See you in a few," I said.

I was back at the North Woods within the hour. Michael and I drank all afternoon, skipped lunch, and went to other bars Michael liked. This was his circuit. Everyone always greeted him, and he introduced me around. He knew I liked country music, and at one bar he gave the bartender a few bills to play all the country songs they had in the jukebox.

At six o'clock, I told Michael I had to go home to see my kids. He asked me out for later that night.

"There's a piano player at the North Woods you've got to hear," he pleaded. I had been ready to call it a day, but it felt good to have an invitation. I went home, showered and changed for the evening, made dinner for the kids, then headed back out.

The North Woods was a whole new ball game at night. The room was almost full, and a hostess was at Michael's side in seconds to lead us to his "night table." Over drinks, I learned about Michael's life. He'd left home at seventeen to go to Las Vegas with hopes of finding more than he could have in his coal-mining town near Pittsburgh. He worked as a waiter and played a lot of poker, sometimes for as many as twelve hours a day.

Now that he lived in Los Angeles, he liked to spend a week in Vegas every month and stay at the Golden Nugget hotel. He asked me to join him in a couple of weeks. He'd get a driver for the limo, and we'd have a hell of a time. I told him I'd love to go but that I'd have to find someone to watch my kids—I couldn't leave them alone for a whole week. He offered me money for a babysitter, and I thanked him but refused.

If I accepted the money, I thought he'd think he'd always need to pay for a babysitter and wouldn't think I was fun anymore.

Around midnight, I followed Michael to his house, which was only two blocks away from the North Woods. This time, I agreed to a tour of Michael's house. It looked stuck in the sixties, with green shag carpeting, a grand piano, a grandfather clock, and wood paneling. There was a large eerie painting of a screaming clown that hung right above the fireplace.

We sat at the kitchen table with an entire chocolate cake while I listened to stories about how he'd managed alone here since his wife of thirty years died from cancer ten years earlier. He had called his wife Madame Queen.

Didn't he call me Madame Queen the other night? I asked him why he called her that.

"Because she was the most wonderful woman and I loved her very much," he replied.

It was getting late, so I thanked Michael for a wonderful day.

"You can stay if you'd like," he said. "So you don't have to drive."

"No, I'm fine to drive, really," I assured him. I stood and gave him a hug and a kiss on the cheek.

"Can I call you tomorrow?" he asked.

"I hope you will," I said.

Driving home, I had to smile. I had gone to the North Woods

to find a boyfriend and to keep my work a secret, and so far, fortune seemed right here in my corner.

Chapter Thirteen
Club 2nd

"I've got something for you," Michael called from his coat closet. He held up a stunning three-quarter-length fur coat. "This was Madame Queen's," he said, beaming. "I want you to have it."

Why was he giving me his dead wife's coat? It felt weird, and it kind of hurt my feelings. Was he pretending I was her? Maybe he didn't think I was worth a new one. I wished he'd given me my own. I wanted to feel special. He shook the coat to urge me into it and I slipped it on, feeling its weight and fullness.

Michael was officially my boyfriend, and the North Woods was my new home away from home. I met Michael there every day at noon for a couple of hours, and then we made the rounds at his other haunts. I visited his house, but I never stayed overnight. Even though the kids were old enough to stay home alone, it was important to me that they knew that their mother was there when they got up in the morning. I didn't want them to feel abandoned like I did when my mom was gone when I woke up in the morning.

Michael slipped the coat off me and draped it over the back of his armchair. He sat on the bed and turned off the light.

"Come over here," he purred.

We had sex, though we never went all the way, probably because of the alcohol in his system. I didn't care. I wasn't especially interested anyway; I was still numb. I didn't feel a thing when he tried to please me, though I acted like I did.

Michael dozed off, and I got up and got dressed. I took my luxurious gift back from the armchair and draped it over my arm, and Michael stirred.

"What are you doing?" he mumbled. "Oh, no, no, no," he scolded, jumping out of bed and taking the coat from my arms. "This coat stays here. It'll always be here when you want to wear it."

I was hurt, but I held back from saying anything. The coat was still his wife's, the real Madame Queen.

For years, Michael went to Las Vegas one week a month, from early Sunday morning to early Friday morning. I'd been tempted to go with him, but I was wary about leaving the kids for five days straight. By the end of the summer, though, the kids had been spending a lot of time on their own, and things had been fine so far, so I figured it would be okay. I thought Popeye, who'd just turned eighteen, and Dawn, at sixteen, were old enough to be home without me, and Rocky could stay with a friend. I'd make sure the refrigerator was stocked with food and make them promise to take good care of themselves and the apartment. So I told Michael I would join him.

Michael hired a limo driver so we could travel in style, sitting in the back, drinking to our hearts' content. I hadn't been this excited since my mom rented the summer beach house so many years earlier.

Our first trip to Vegas was the Sunday after Labor Day. The four-hour ride took us through the Mojave Desert, where the sands were smooth and beautiful in the sunshine. I felt so free.

"The bar's open!" Michael called out at 9:30 a.m. He reached into the cooler for a couple of cold beers. I had only started drinking this early a few times in my life, and always to cure a hangover. But what the hell? Vacation had started.

As we pulled into the parking lot at the Golden Nugget, two valets greeted us like we were royalty and helped us out onto a red carpet.

"Take our bags to 1530," Michael requested.

I frowned. "You don't know this about me yet," I said. "I'm afraid of heights."

"You're kidding," he said. "I thought you weren't afraid of anything."

Thank God we had already started drinking.

"I'll tell you what," he said, "let's start at the bar."

Just like back home, Michael greeted the bartenders by name and shook hands like they were old friends. We drank beer and watched the tourists come and go while I got used to the feeling of timelessness. People stayed up all night here, losing money, making money, selling sex, buying sex, running away from home for as long as they could.

By noon, Michael asked if I was ready (read: buzzed enough) to go up to our room. Even after all the beer I had, the thought of an elevator ride to the fifteenth floor freaked me out. But somehow I made it to the fifteenth floor without panicking, and we navigated the long hall to room 1530.

We were in a suite! I went inside and looked around, counting six telephones (including one in each bathroom), two wet bars, and a breathtaking city view with a skyline of mountains. I did my best to act nonchalant, like I'd done anything like this before.

I quickly unzipped my garment bag and put on my cowboy hat.

"I need a cowboy hat for the concert we're going to tomorrow night," Michael said.

"Who are we seeing?" I asked excitedly.

"Willie Nelson," he said.

I fell onto the couch and squealed. I jumped up and threw my arms around him. Willie Nelson was my favorite. Michael was show-ing me the time of my life.

At four o'clock, Michael took his nap. He was a man of routine. Every afternoon, he took a two-hour nap to rest up for the night. I lay next to Michael, but all I could think about was Stephanie. We hadn't talked in years, not because we'd had a falling out or anything but because we just had busy lives. It seemed strange to call her now and tell her I was only half an hour away. She would want to come out with us, and I knew it wouldn't work. Michael didn't need an old friend of mine stealing his show. I decided not to call her, but I was restless.

After Michael woke up from his nap, we had a long night at the casino. At six o'clock the next morning, I woke up with a raging hangover. Michael was snoring and I couldn't go back to sleep. The only way I could feel better and be in good spirits by the time Michael got up was to have a drink. I sat on the couch and opened one beer after another. I finished a six-pack and felt slightly normal again.

That day, every hour led me closer to Willie. After Michael's afternoon nap, I put on my sexy lace top, Levi's, boots, and cowboy hat and Madame Queen's fur coat. I had a plan, and I needed to look great for it.

"I'm going onstage to get his autograph," I confided to Michael as we took our seats in the theater. We were eight rows from the stage.

The concert was amazing, and when Willie announced his last song, I got up and walked toward the stage like I belonged on it. No one said a word as I made my way up the steps and joined people in the wings. I whispered hello to them like I'd been backstage a hun-dred times before. I waited there through the encore, and when the curtain started to close, I walked right up to Willie.

"I'm a big fan of yours," I said, giving him my warmest smile. "And I just snuck onstage to get your autograph."

"Well, how about that," he replied kindly. "And what's your name?"

He signed his autograph on my Golden Nugget notepad and tipped his hat. Willie Nelson was the biggest highlight of our trip.

When I got home from Vegas, just a week before school started, the inevitable happened: the landlord gave us thirty days' notice. Having teenagers with friends coming and going all hours of the day meant there was no way to keep the noise down.

Michael stepped up and helped me find a house—a big four-bedroom, three-bath house on Second Avenue in Arcadia, with a game room out back, a large patio, and a two-car garage. I didn't have the cash to get us into this house, and there was no way I could have rented it with my credit rating, but Michael used his name for the credit check, paid the first month's rent and the security deposit, and cosigned the lease with me. I was so grateful.

I made the place ours as soon as we moved in. I painted and wallpapered every room and turned the patio into a play space where the kids could entertain friends, complete with a Ping-Pong table, pool table, and bar. I made a sign that read CLUB 2ND, with room for the kids' friends to sign their names, like a guest book. From then on, the house was officially called Club 2nd.

Popeye and Dawn drank with their friends, but they were good kids, and I turned a blind eye. I knew they cut school occasionally, but I understood. Teens did that. I believed they would outgrow it and do better.

Rocky was another story. One day, I saw him through the slightly open door of his room smoking a joint. My heart sank. He was only thirteen years old. I remembered being thirteen when I had my first drink, and now I could see how young I really was.

It wasn't that I was opposed to punishment; I just wanted to be sure the punishment fit the crime. Punishing Rocky too hard could put a wedge between us, and I wanted him to feel like he could talk to me about anything. We had always been buddies. I grounded him for two days.

"Don't worry, Mom. I only tried it this once. The other guys are smoking, not me," he explained.

"All right," I said. "Clean up the kitchen and you won't be grounded."

We'd been through this routine before. I'd start off with a plan, and I'd end up telling him he was a good person and reminding him of all the good things he did. I cared more about building him up with love than grounding him and making him feel like he'd done something wrong. It was just my way: show my children love and hope for the best.

* * *

One day that fall, I was at Michael's house, and he asked me to come to the front door. He said, "A beautiful blonde like you belongs in a classy car like this." He opened the door and pointed to a gorgeous black Cadillac Seville with red leather interior. It was a 1977, my favorite model.

"Is this for me?" I asked.

He smiled, nodded, and handed me the keys. I loved it, and I couldn't wait to drive it.

With Dawn and Rocky back in school and Popeye in his first semester of college, I started going to Las Vegas with Michael every month. To cut costs (or maybe because he didn't feel like he had to impress me anymore), Michael started driving the limo each way himself. He thought it was a waste of money to pay for a driver's hotel and meals. I didn't mind. I got to sit in the passenger compartment, stretch out my legs, listen to music, and drink cold beers. Michael had recently customized the seat so it could turn into a bed. I kicked back on it and enjoyed the view.

That December, though work was still steady, I was more aware than ever of how the rent at our new house was over my head. I had already rented out the studio at the back of the house, which had its own kitchen, bathroom, and entrance, to help with the bills (unbeknownst to Michael—I figured he didn't need to know everything). But raising three teenagers as a single mom was just plain expensive. And I wanted this house more than anything.

By Christmas, I had a solution. I would find another renter to live in Rocky's bedroom, which had its own entrance and bathroom. Rocky would get the garage, which was separate from the house, and I'd set him up with a TV, stereo, bed, and couch. It was cold in there, but he didn't care. It was private and he had lots of room for his friends.

Rocky and his friends were drinking, smoking pot, and inhaling nitrous oxide. Every time I found evidence of it, I would send his friends home and tell Rocky never to do it again. Then my pager would beep, and I'd tell him I had to go show a house. Everything seemed out of control around me. I wanted to quit drinking and have life become more manageable, but all I could do was wish for it.

One day, not long after I'd rented out Rocky's bedroom, the phone rang. I answered it.

"I have to move," said the voice on the other line. "Because of some problems."

It was Stephanie. I was surprised to hear her voice; we hadn't spoken in a few years.

"What kinds of problems?" I asked.

"Physical problems. And emotional problems. Trust me. I have to get out of here," she said.

"Girl, you know I'm here for you. Come to LA as soon as you'd like. We can share my king-size bed."

The next week, Stephanie was standing on my doorstep.

Chapter Fourteen
Make It Official

Stephanie looked older, but I probably looked older too—we were in our forties, for God's sake. Her eyes had lost their sparkle. I remembered those brown eyes of hers being full of mischief. Now she just looked worn-out.

"I got some tests done a few years ago to try to figure out what was up with those bad headaches, but they couldn't find anything," she confided. "And the headaches wouldn't stop. You know I never used to take drugs, right?"

I listened.

"One day I went to my friend and said, 'Just gimme some.' I was pain free for the first time in years," she said.

Stephanie was still hooked on heroin. She'd quit a few times, sometimes at rehab, sometimes on her own, but she'd never stopped completely.

"So what's next?" I asked.

"I'm going to stay in LA," she said. "I don't know anyone here besides you. I'm not going to use here."

"You mean you're quitting while you're here?" I confirmed.

"No, I'm taking a break. I'll only use once a month, when I go to Vegas to pick up my check. You know, leave it at home."

"I don't know, Stephanie. They say cold turkey's the only way," I told her.

"You drink," she replied with a smile.

"I drink," I agreed.

"Then you understand," she said.

I did understand, but I still felt uneasy about it. Nevertheless, it was great having my best friend around again. Having another adult in the house was good too. I didn't feel so bad about staying overnight at Michael's with Stephanie at home, and I started staying there a few nights a week.

I'd sleep at Michael's, go home in the morning to check on things, and meet Michael at the North Woods at noon. If I had a call, I would see a client and then go home to see the kids. Sometimes I'd make a simple dinner, but usually we weren't all there at the same time, so we'd fend for ourselves. At seven o'clock, I was back at Michael's for another night out. The kids had parties on the weekends, but I figured Stephanie could handle it. And in truth, I was drinking more than ever and didn't care much about what anyone else needed.

My kids were busy with their lives. I was lonely. Michael didn't like coming over; he didn't want anything to do with kids. He liked his routine and his privacy. I was different. I wanted someone to share my life with under the same roof with my kids. I wanted to feel needed. I was stuck in the middle, staying at Michael's a few nights a week and drinking, chasing away the desire for more.

* * *

Five months had passed since Stephanie moved in, and I started to notice strange things going on. Instead of watching TV all day, she would get busy with a project—like cleaning a crystal chandelier she found at a garage sale—and stay at it for hours. The day I saw her nodding off in front of the TV, I knew what was happening.

"You're right," she admitted. "I broke my rule."

She was using heroin again. Here in LA. I didn't like it, but I knew how hard it was to kick a habit—wasn't I drinking again after a short break just the month before?

Not long after that unfortunate discovery, Michael made an unfortunate discovery of his own. We were sitting in his "office" reading the newspaper when my pager beeped.

"I've got to show a house," I said. "I'll be back in an hour."

Michael didn't look up. "You know where to find me," he said.

That was Michael, always understanding about my having to leave suddenly for work, even in the middle of lunch. He acted like it was no big deal, and it wasn't. The motel was two blocks away, and I was never gone long.

But that day was different. When I got back to the North Woods, Michael set down his drink and looked me right in the eyes.

"You weren't showing a house, were you? You're a prostitute," he said.

I sucked in my breath.

"Is that a question?" I asked.

"Did it sound like one?" he asked.

"You're right, Michael," I admitted. "I'm trying to make a living. I didn't want you to know about it because I didn't think you'd approve."

"I do know," he said. "I've known for a long time."

"Why haven't you said anything before?" I asked him.

He shrugged. "I know the life."

"The life?" I asked.

"I used to be a pimp," he said. "In Vegas."

"What?" I exclaimed. "You were a pimp?!"

I couldn't believe what I was hearing. I thought pimps were sleazebags, guys dressed in loud clothes with gold chains around their necks. Michael did not fit this mold, and because he didn't feel like a pimp, I decided to believe he was a respectable man.

Michael told me his story. He had played poker for a few years in Vegas and hung out at the Golden Nugget. He got involved with running girls out of the hotel. He said, "My life is different now, better, and I want to keep it that way." Then he said he'd seen me driving my Cadillac across town. "I knew you weren't going to show a house," he said, and his voice cracked. "It hurt to know, because I've fallen in love with you."

I shook my head. This was exactly what I didn't want to hear, exactly the reason I never wanted another boyfriend to know what I did for a living. It was too much to deal with.

"I'm asking you to quit," he said gently.

I couldn't believe what I was hearing.

"Quit completely. Quit now," he insisted.

"Michael, you're asking a lot," I told him.

"I know I am."

"I don't have another way to support my family," I said.

"You'll be fine. Quitting the business means freedom. Look, I have a great idea. I'll hire a driver. We'll drive up to Morro Bay, and you can throw your pager into the ocean, make it official."

This was really stretching me.

"We'll make a vacation out of it. I know a great hotel with a million-dollar view," he said.

He asked if I could be ready to leave that Saturday at 9:00 a.m. Before I could answer, he said he would take me to a Prostitutes Anonymous meeting too; he knew of one in Hollywood. They'd been a big help when he quit pimping. He'd been waiting for the right time to bring it up.

What in the world was I going to do? I could toss the pager into the ocean, but I'd have to replace it right away. I had to support myself and my family, but I couldn't imagine life without him. I decided to play along to appease him. I'd have a new pager ordered by morning, and I'd figure out how to keep it a secret.

All the way home, my mind buzzed with worry. I'd have to play the role of a reformed prostitute so he wouldn't suspect anything. I would get a copy of a song we liked by Billy Ray Cyrus, "She's Not Cryin' Anymore," and I'd tell him I'd think of the day I quit the business every time I heard it. He couldn't be suspicious with that kind of sentimentality.

By the next morning, I had a plan. There were more lies to keep track of than ever, but it was all I could do. I would tell Michael that Stephanie was going to start paying rent, and since he didn't know I had someone renting out the studio, I'd tell him I was going to find someone to move in. With that, I felt he would believe that I could handle the rent without working.

On Saturday, I was ready to perform when the limo pulled up in front of my house. I climbed in holding my pager and sat down next to Michael. He was beaming.

"I'm so proud of you, Patty Sue," he said. "You're doing the right thing."

I wished I'd never told him my full name. He gave me a kiss.

"I love you," I said, which really meant, *Do you love me?* He didn't say it back. That always hurt so much.

I handed him the Billy Ray Cyrus cassette. He put it in the player and hit play, and we popped open a couple of beers to toast to the big event.

When Morro Rock came into view, Michael told the driver to pull over. I cupped my pager in my hands.

"This is the end of a long relationship," I said, taking Michael's hand. Michael actually teared up, and I did too. Talk about getting caught up in the drama.

Michael waited in the limo while I walked out to the shoreline, took a last look at the pager, and raised my arm. I threw the little plastic device as far as I could and watched it disappear into the waves; then I went back to the limo, where Michael handed me another beer.

"She Ain't Cryin' Anymore" was playing, and Michael cranked up the volume.

At that moment, the lyrics meant everything he wished for me: that I would feel good about myself and accept only the good I deserved. But my tears were for reasons Michael could never have guessed.

Later that week, Michael took me to my first PA meeting. You weren't supposed to have any alcohol before going, so we made sure to use breath mints.

Michael and I pulled our chairs into a close circle, and everyone told their story of how they had gotten into the business and why they had quit. This was the first time this group had had a man at the meeting, but everyone was welcoming to Michael, who introduced himself as a former pimp. He shared how one of his girls had become severely depressed because of her work and had committed suicide. That was the end of his pimping career. He said that he was here to support me.

When my turn came, I told my story—how it all started, Bert, my car breaking down. It was interesting to listen to the other women's stories. They had different backgrounds and had earned different amounts of money. One woman took home fifteen hundred dollars for an all-nighter. I only made sixty dollars an hour. It never even occurred to me that I could have been charging more.

All of the women had one thing in common: it was hard to quit because of the lost income. We had gotten into the business to make money, and the bills had to be paid even during the transition to a regular job.

On the way home, Michael and I talked about the women and their stories. I was happy for them that they had the will to keep going when times got hard. Each one had another form of income now, but they needed the meetings because they knew it would be easy to slide back into easy money.

"I'll go there with you every week if you want," Michael offered. I thanked him, but inside I was screaming. Every week? What had I gotten myself into?

* * *

After that weekend, it wasn't business as usual anymore. I had to hide my new pager in the car whenever I was with Michael. I missed a lot of calls. When I finally returned a page, it was usually too late. It was hard.

I went to a few more PA meetings, until the night Michael announced he thought I didn't need them anymore. He believed I was making enough money by renting out the rooms in Club 2nd.

"You're doing just fine," he told me over drinks. We toasted.

Chapter Fifteen
Don't Touch Me

I was living a double life. When I was with the kids, I was in real estate. I answered my pager and went on calls. When I was with Michael, my pager was off.

I wondered about our relationship. Where was it going? We had been seeing each other for nearly a year, and there was no talk of a future together. We just went day to day, doing the rounds, having a good time and nothing more. One night after the North Woods, Michael and I went back to his house.

"We've been dating for almost a year, and we've never talked about getting married," I began. I was hiding behind the bottle, and I knew it. Michael started to speak, but I interrupted him to avoid rejection. "It doesn't even have to be a real diamond. It can be a cubic zirconia."

Michael looked relieved. "If a ring is what you want, I know just the place," he said, raising his glass to me with a smile.

I was stunned. It wasn't a marriage proposal, but it was something.

A day later at the breakfast table, Michael patted the chair beside him.

"Patty Sue," he said, "come sit down." He sounded so businesslike.

The moment I sat down, he pulled a ring box out of his pocket and opened it to show me a big, glittering solitaire. He held my left hand gently in his.

"I, Michael A. Conner, am engaging Patty Sue Frankhouser," he said. He slipped the ring onto my finger.

"Oh, Michael! It's so beautiful!" I cried, holding up my hand.

"You did say it could be a CZ," he confirmed.

"I don't care if it isn't a diamond. What matters is we're engaged!" I exclaimed.

He put a finger to my lips.

"This will be our secret. No one ever needs to know," he told me.

"Isn't this an engagement ring?" I asked, puzzled.

He gave me a quick peck on the lips and stood to leave.

As his car pulled out of the driveway, I spread my fingers wide to admire the ring. But I didn't feel as happy as I thought I would. I truly didn't care that it wasn't a diamond. But the way he'd given it to me wasn't the least bit romantic. At the breakfast table? "I, Michael A. Conner, am engaging Patty Sue Frankhouser"? Come on. It's so weird. Why did he use my maiden name? I guess Michael was a unique sort of man; he did things his own way. When I got home, I showed Stephanie.

"It's so big!" she cried. "Is it real?"

"You're the only person I'm telling, Stephanie. It's a CZ."

"The cheap bastard!" she exclaimed. "Can't he fork over some cash to buy you a real engagement ring?"

"It is a real engagement ring," I said. "I told him he could get me a CZ."

"He can afford a diamond," she argued.

"I know," I said. "But this is just as pretty, and who can tell the difference? You couldn't."

Stephanie shrugged. "Real's real. You know what fake is."

Later that day, Dawn, Popeye, and Rocky came home. Dawn said the ring was beautiful. Popeye and Rocky said it was big.

"When are you getting married again, Mom?" Rocky asked.

"We don't have a date yet, but we will," I told him. It sounded as casual as the whole thing felt.

We weren't going to move into Michael's, that much I knew. He always said his house was only big enough for two, which made me sad to hear, but I tried to make it okay by reminding myself that it had nothing to do with how he felt about my kids. The truth is, I never once thought about what being married to Michael would look like. Michael didn't do family. He never talked with his sisters or his brother. He said that when he'd left Pennsylvania, he'd left everybody, and that's how he wanted to keep it.

When Michael and I made our rounds to the bars, I showed off my ring. If anyone asked about the wedding date, Michael always changed the subject. I never pressed him about it when we were alone because I knew he wasn't ready for marriage. But he was devoted to me, and I had the ring to show it. That was enough for him, so it had to be enough for me.

* * *

A few months later, change hit, and it hit hard. I decided I was sick and tired of being sick and tired. I was done with being drunk and hungover. I was especially done with not remembering what I did or said. How would I ever understand the pain I caused my family if I couldn't even remember how awful I acted?

So far, any attempts I had made to quit drinking had backfired. I usually started drinking earlier in the day out of fear of getting sober. I was afraid of how I'd feel, that I wouldn't be able to handle it, that I'd be nervous all the time, that my panic attacks and phobias would come back. Every time I tried to quit drinking, I asked myself why I always started again, why I always had that first drink. The answer was that even if it was for a short time, the pain went away. I had some relief.

But this time, I was ready. I told the kids I was quitting. And I told Michael I would be staying at home for a few days.

The day I quit, I stayed busy by painting and redecorating the kitchen. At 3:00 p.m., I still didn't want a drink, although I did start to feel a little edgy. Dawn and I were going shopping, and the thought of it made me nervous. I decided I needed just a little something to take the edge off, so I went out and bought a small wine cooler. If I didn't get any more to drink, I figured I wasn't really an alcoholic.

Dawn and I ended up having a good time, and on the way home, we stopped for a bite to eat. She asked how I was feeling.

"I'm fine," I told her, which was true. I didn't want anything to drink.

That night, I was almost asleep in bed when I heard one of Popeye's friends.

"I'm making a liquor run!" he shouted. "Anyone want anything?"

I sat straight up in bed and said, "I do!"

In seconds, I was out of bed and going through my purse for money. I told him to get me a bottle of wine, red or white, it didn't matter. Then I turned on the bedroom light and waited, never once thinking about my decision to quit. When he got back, I went to my bedroom, closed the door, and drank the entire bottle. When it was empty, I went to the store to get another one.

I don't remember anything after that. Except that my hangover lasted for days.

I was addicted to alcohol. I had known this since I was in the hospital for alcoholism in 1984, and here I was, ten years later, still trying to find ways to prove to myself that I wasn't. Now I was really depressed. I had been so sure I could quit. I told myself I would try again as soon as I was up to it. Michael and I were going to Vegas the next week, so I wasn't going to start just yet. Vegas wasn't exactly the best place to quit drinking.

In Vegas that week, I learned something about Michael: his real age. I had suspected for a long time that he was more than ten years older than me, like he'd said he was. He used a cane now because his gait was unsteady. He gave me his driver's license so that I could place a bet for him at a sports bar. I glanced at it while I was in line, and there it was—he was born in 1928, twenty years before I was born. No wonder he liked music from the thirties and forties. No wonder people asked me if he was my father. I decided not to tell Michael that I knew. I didn't want him to feel bad for thinking he had to lie about it.

After that Vegas trip, it was time to really quit drinking. This time I decided I would go cold turkey, which meant I would stay home for a week instead of doing the bar circuit with Michael.

It was awful. I was nervous. Everything bothered me. I was snappy. And for the first time in my life, I understood how my mom had felt when she tried to quit drinking. I really got her.

One night, I walked outside to get some fresh air and noticed cigarette butts all over the driveway, patio, and front yard. I couldn't believe the kids' friends tossed their butts in our yard like it was a big ashtray. I got a flashlight and sat down outside to wait for the kids to come home. Rocky was first.

"Go get a grocery bag," I ordered him, "and pick up every last one of these butts." I shined the flashlight. "Do it now!"

Dawn was next. When she came up, I shined the flashlight on her. "Look at this mess!" I shouted. "Put down your things and clean this up right now!"

They weren't used to me even noticing the butts, but I was sober now and I noticed everything. The next day, when I saw their friends at the house, I told them not to come over anymore. "You can never have a party here again," I said sternly. My hands were shaking. I'd wanted this house to be a family home where the kids could find a soft place to land and feel safe and secure and loved, but because of my drinking, I had allowed it to devolve into chaos. I saw clearly now that my children and I were sharing our home with not only the kids' friends but also three other adults—my two renters plus Stephanie—and it broke my heart to realize that I hadn't given them a real home. Instead, I'd given them a frat house.

And then, before I knew it, I was drinking again—and drunk. It was late at night, and I was telling Stephanie what a wretched mess everything was.

"Being sober drove me crazy!" I shouted. "What is so freakin' hard about taking out the damn trash?" I marched into the kitchen and started throwing all of the dirty dishes into the overflowing trash can.

Stephanie was high on heroin. "If I were you," she mumbled, "I'd do something now before things get worse. Why don't you take that trash can and empty it on Dawn?"

"She's sleeping," I told her.

"If you don't make a big statement, this shit will go on forever," she said.

"Really?"

"Just do it."

I believed Stephanie was right. I had asked Dawn to take out the trash that morning, and it was still there! I took the dishes out of the trash can, picked it up, opened Dawn's bedroom door, and stepped inside. In one single motion, I dumped the entire contents of the trash can on her while she slept.

"What in the hell are you doing?!" she screamed, her arms flailing as pieces of uneaten food cascaded down on her. There were cereal boxes, watermelon rinds, corn chips, candy wrappers, and much more.

"I'm reminding you to take out the trash!" I said, shaking the empty container to get out the last bits.

"Get out of here! Get out of my room!" she screamed.

I rushed to my bedroom, where Stephanie waited.

"Good for you, girlfriend," she reassured me. "Things will change, you'll see. This is tough love. Sometimes you just have to do it."

The next morning, Dawn was seated at the breakfast table eating a bowl of cereal. She didn't look up when I came in.

"Good morning, sweetheart," I said, trying to put my arms around her shoulders.

She jerked away. "Don't touch me!"

I shrunk back. I went to my bedroom to find Stephanie.

"Dawn's freaked out," I said. "Any idea why?"

Stephanie rolled her eyes. "Of course she's freaked out. You don't remember?"

I sat still and let the memory drift in. Garbage raining down on my beautiful daughter asleep in her bed? Did I really do that?

I went to Dawn's bedroom and cautiously opened the door. She was in front of her closet, choosing what to wear for the day.

"Dawn, I'm sorry," I said. "That was stupid. I was drunk."

She didn't turn around.

"I asked you to take out the trash, and you didn't do it. I was so frustrated that no one cleans up around here. I'm sorry I took it out on you," I said.

She finally looked at me. "I get it," she said. "But what you did was stupid."

"I'm really sorry, honey. Will you forgive me?" I pleaded.

"Yes, I forgive you, but don't ever do it again," she said.

"I won't," I told her. "I promise. Not ever." I took her into my arms. I hoped she could let it go.

It would be twenty-two more years before *I* finally did.

Chapter Sixteen
Sick

I still felt horrible about what I'd done to Dawn. It made me sick to think about, and of course it's all I could think about. It was different between us now. I grew afraid of her not loving me. The idea of conflict with her intimidated me because she was so self-assured. If she didn't do what I asked, I didn't do anything. I wanted to be a perfect mom. If only I'd had a voice when I was sober, I could have confronted her differently. But I didn't. I realized I was afraid of myself. Of who I became when I was drinking. Of being my mother's daughter.

I decided to quit drinking again. I wondered if this was how my mother felt about how she treated me. Maybe that's why I never got grounded. Maybe she was afraid I wouldn't love her too. Maybe she didn't love herself.

Stephanie's forty-sixth birthday was a week away, and I wanted to do something special for her. I decided to splurge and surprise her with a limo ride to dinner at Spago, the movie-star hangout on Sunset Boulevard.

I wasn't sure Michael would loan me his limo just to go out with Stephanie, so I told him I wanted to take her and her parents out to dinner. That sounded more respectable, and he could be sure I wouldn't mess things up by drinking. I was nervous about lying, but it worked. He thought it was a great idea and offered to get me his driver.

On the day of Stephanie's birthday, I started to stress. I called an old neighbor who was a waiter at Spago and asked him if we could be seated in his serving area. I told him that when I ordered a Diet Coke, he should make sure there was a double shot of rum in it.

"And don't spill a word to my friend about it," I added. "I don't want her worrying about me. I'm only drinking just this one."

He said he would do it. Everything would be fine.

On Saturday afternoon, the limo pulled up to the house, and Stephanie was surprised.

"Get in, birthday girl!" I shouted. "We are going to have one hell of a night on the town, just the two of us!"

Right away, I made Stephanie her favorite drink, Kahlúa and milk. I felt desire shudder through me. I couldn't wait to get to the restaurant and order my Diet Coke.

The second we were seated at the restaurant, I ordered our drinks. As soon as the drinks arrived, I grabbed my Diet Coke and emptied the glass in seconds. Ah. My tummy felt warm. I motioned for our waiter.

"Another Diet Coke, please," I said. He hesitated. "Thank you," I said, with a look and a nod.

But Stephanie knew me and my tricks. "I know you're drinking, Patty," she said.

"What are you talking about? I'm having a couple of Diet Cokes," I said defensively.

She laughed. "Every time your mom quit, we knew she was drinking the minute she took a few sips of just about anything," she said. "You're just like her."

I let that sink in. "It's hard being sober, Stephanie. I wanted tonight to be fun," I told her.

Stephanie reached across the table and squeezed my hand. "It is fun. Thank you for this."

Stephanie was right. I was my mother's daughter. Whenever my mom started drinking, she thought I didn't notice. But I always knew, because her personality changed that quick. Maybe there was a part of me that thought I could get away with it too. All I wanted was another drink.

In no time, my drunk personality was in full force. I jumped the second I recognized a movie star come in, and I couldn't even remember his name. Before he could even sit down, I walked right up to him, gave him a big hug, and thanked him for being such a good friend all these years. Stephanie couldn't stop laughing.

We went to our driver outside and told him that we were going to walk to a club across the street and page him when we were ready to be picked up. Hours later, we came out of the club smashed and climbed into the limo. The driver told us it was after 1:00 a.m. and that Michael had been paging him.

"Absolutely do not call him!" I ordered. "I'm in charge!"

The night was a blur after the second club. We cruised Hollywood while playing music, laughing, and drinking. Because we were drinking so much, we had to pee. We were barely moving in the traffic, so we told the driver to turn on a side street so we could get out and squat in the bushes. We both fell onto our butts and were covered in mud.

It was 5:00 a.m. when we dropped Stephanie off at home. She could barely walk. When we got to Michael's, the driver helped me out of the limo, but I fell into the bushes and ripped my pants. Michael was livid.

"I've been up all night!" he shouted.

The last thing I remember was sitting on the bathroom floor, throwing up, trying to take off my muddy, torn clothes. I woke up sick as a dog. I could hardly walk. I apologized to Michael and promised I would never drink again. He offered to get a nurse to come and be with me while he was gone, but I refused. I'd gotten myself into this, and I didn't think I deserved a nurse. I knew he was upset, and I didn't want him paying for someone to take care of me.

He left at eleven thirty and headed for the North Woods as usual. Lying in bed, I could feel my heart pounding. It felt like it was shaking. I reached for a glass of water, and my hand trembled so badly that the water spilled. I was cold one minute and sweating the next, soaking the bed. I regretted not accepting a nurse. I was alone and scared.

When Michael finally came home, he brought hot soup from the North Woods and helped me to the table. I picked up the spoon, but my hand was shaking so badly that I couldn't possibly bring it to my mouth. Michael took the spoon from me and fed me the soup.

He helped me back to bed, and the days wore on. Dawn called one day to ask for a ride to work because her car had broken down.

"Your mother's quitting drinking," I heard Michael tell her. "She's not feeling too well, but she'll be better soon."

All I could think was that I was a pathetic mother and that I didn't deserve to have such a sweet daughter. She needed her mother, and I couldn't even help her. She'd never believe me. *She thinks I'm a drunk*, I told myself. *She thinks I don't care. I hate myself.*

For five days I stayed in bed, detoxing. While I lay there—sick for every minute of it—I decided that no matter what, I would never drink again. I wrote down everything I was feeling so I would never forget what drinking was doing to me and my family.

The date of my last drink was Saturday, September 3, 1994. I was forty-six years old. I wrote: *Beer or wine or any alcoholic drink is poison to me. There is never a time when I can say I will just have a couple of beers because I always make that stretch out until I am a blacked-out, self-destructive, drunk bitch. I will be sick, maybe dead. My heart will pound and shake. I will salivate and have the dry heaves. I will always hurt the ones I love.*

My note helped me to remember that my addiction was not stronger than I was, not stronger than who I wanted to be. It could only win if I let it. Writing my note helped me stay aware of the consequences of choosing to drink. By reading it every day, my note helped me make the decision not to. I was now on the path of making conscious choices.

I put my note on the bathroom wall at Michael's house and on the back of the bathroom door at mine. I saw it and read it every time I went to the bathroom. I kept a copy of it in my car. I read it from start to finish several times every day. The kids were very supportive and read my note every time they went into my bathroom. Before long, they had it memorized.

After a few weeks, I was feeling a little better. When the time came for me and Michael to plan our monthly Vegas trip, I told him I had to bring a copy of my note and put it on the bathroom wall at the hotel. He understood and was very supportive. I made it through the trip without drinking, but it was very hard because I didn't think I was fun anymore. I couldn't relax; I was aware I was not the life of the party, and it was hard for me to keep up with Michael's routine. I tried meditating, but it made me feel like I was going to suffocate. I would try to breathe slowly and evenly, but focusing on each breath made me feel like I might not be able to get the next breath, and I would panic. I had to find a way to relax.

* * *

Things were different now that I wasn't drinking. To handle stress, I watched a lot of TV and ate more sweets than ever. I bought cookies, brownies, candy, and ice cream. At least I wasn't drinking.

Matinees were my great escape. I didn't have to take beer with me anymore. I ate candy and popcorn and drank Diet Coke. I liked seeing movies by myself. Especially in an empty theater.

My favorite TV show was *The Oprah Winfrey Show*. I was learning so much. I read books some of her guests had written, and I recorded some of the shows so I could watch them again and again. I discovered Gary Zukav's brilliant book *The Seat of the Soul*, and it put me on the path to understanding my soul and authentic power. I also discovered Iyanla Vanzant, who taught me that life is better when you center it on what's happening inside you, not what's happening around you.

I was still working—though I was down to only a few clients a week—but the work was harder for me. Now that I was sober, I wasn't as detached as I had been before. I was becoming more self-aware.

* * *

A month after I quit drinking, Stephanie asked if her brother, Buzz, could stay with us. As much as I didn't want another person sleeping under our roof, I wanted to do right by my friend, so I told her he could stay for a short while and sleep on the floor at the foot of our bed until he could find a place of his own.

Right away, I found out that Buzz was using heroin too. Every day, he and Stephanie would get high and watch TV in the bedroom. I hated it. I knew they weren't going to quit until they really wanted to. One day, I discovered I was missing some money and jewelry. I didn't say anything about it to anyone, but I was on alert. As the weeks went by, I found that I could put cash in my dresser drawer and find it gone as soon as the next day. Michael had given me Madame Queen's jewelry, which also disappeared. Who could I suspect besides Stephanie and Buzz? But I couldn't say anything. I had no proof.

For six months, every day was a challenge. I had a thirty-three-year habit to break. Reading my note every day was a big help. Whenever I felt my heart racing, I'd remember to breathe, then sit down and think about what to do next so I wouldn't end up at the liquor store. As soon as I had a handle on what was happening, I would go and read my note. Every time I read it, I remembered how I felt writing those words: sick. Horribly sick. I never wanted to feel that way again. I couldn't go through the pain of it, and I couldn't cause my family that kind of pain anymore. I was done. I had no idea how much harder it was going to get.

In April, almost eight months after my last drink, I got a call from my brother Steve. He was speaking with his usual slur. But something was different this time: I wasn't drunk too. Seeing my brother drunk all the time helped me see how messed up I really was while I was drinking. I didn't realize the damage I was doing to my children because I couldn't remember the awful things I had done. Listening to Steve helped me remember why I'd quit drinking. For years, he would get so drunk that he got the dry heaves. He couldn't keep anything down, not even alcohol. It broke my heart to see him so sick. I had taken him to the emergency room so many times.

"I'm done with this shit," he slurred on the phone that day. "I'm gonna take a bottle of pills and get out."

"Stop it, Steve," I said. "I'm watching a show. You'll be fine." Steve never followed through with his suicidal threats, and there had been many over the years, so I felt okay telling him I couldn't talk. But he called back every five minutes for the next hour. Each time he called, I told him the same thing: "I'm watching my favorite show. I'll call you back when it's over. You'll be fine." About the tenth time he called, I was pissed.

"You've got to stop calling, Steve! Go ahead and take the damn pills if you want to! Put them all in your mouth and drink them down."

He didn't call back. The next day, Evelyn called.

"Is Steve with you?" she asked.

She told me she had been at her mother's since Sunday and that Steve wasn't answering the phone. I immediately knew what that meant and hung up without saying goodbye. I brought Stephanie and Buzz with me to my brother's house, fifteen miles away. I ran up to the door and pounded it with my fist. No answer. I pounded some more.

"Steve!" I yelled. "Are you in there? Steve! It's me, Patty. Are you in there?!" Still no answer. I ran to his next-door neighbor's house to call 911.

The fire department arrived quickly. Two firemen broke the door open and went inside while I waited on the front steps with Stephanie and Buzz, in tears. I didn't want to see. A few minutes later, one of the firemen came out. He put a hand on my shoulder.

"Your brother is dead," he said quietly. I covered my face with my hands. I knew it. I just knew it. If only I'd stayed on the phone with him, if only I'd never said what I did. He was calling out for help, and I wasn't there for him. My brother. He hadn't been fooling around before; he'd just never done it. And now he had. Everyone kept saying it wasn't my fault, that sooner or later my brother was going to kill himself from drinking, whether he took those pills or not. There was nothing I could have done.

At home, I went to my note in the bathroom and stood in front of it. I repeated the first sentence over and over: "Beer or wine or any alcoholic drink is poison to me. Beer or wine or any alcoholic drink is poison to me. Beer or wine or any alcoholic drink is poison to me." I never once took a drink.

A few days later, I put on Steve's Rams cap, the one he wore every day. Suddenly, I felt okay with what I did. He had suffered for so long. It's possible he had been waiting for me to give him permission. Maybe I'd helped him. He had been in so much pain, pain the drinking was never going to take away. The drinking was causing it.

I called my brother Greg in Hawaii. He said he would fly out the next day. It was comforting to know Greg would be at the memorial, that someone who understood would be there.

Michael wasn't going. I wasn't disappointed because I never expected much of him. After all, there was only one Madame Queen, and it was not me.

Chapter Seventeen
My Little Parties

"Let me look at you," I said.

I hardly recognized Greg. My brother, the surfer-turned-Vietnam-vet-turned-Hawaiian-electrician, looked older than I'd remembered. He was a little pudgy with a beer belly, his sandy blond hair was receding, and he wore a beard spotted with gray. It had been nine years since we'd seen each other, but as soon as he spoke, it was like no time had passed at all.

"Patty," he said, grinning. "It's good to see you."

There was almost too much to catch up on. We sat on the patio and reminisced about the good times with our brother—from way back when, before Steve started drinking. No one else had those memories, and it felt good to remember.

With his second beer, Greg raised his bottle for a toast. Then he told me he was an alcoholic. I wasn't surprised. I was one. Steve was one. Mom was one. Our whole family had a drinking problem.

And then he told me that he was schizophrenic. He had been on medication for it for a long time. I remembered how he'd acted when he got back from Vietnam. He was paranoid, and we were sure it was PTSD from combat. It never went away, and it had gotten worse.

"We've all got our battles," I told him, patting his hand.

I told him about Michael. I told him he was twenty years older than me, that we were engaged, the CZ secret. I told him he never came to visit me and that he had no interest in getting to know my kids. And I told him he wouldn't be at Steve's memorial, so it was likely Greg would never meet him.

Greg lit a cigarette. "Life's not always easy," he said.

Steve's memorial was small and outdoors, in the foothills of the San Gabriel Mountains. I put on Steve's Rams cap and jacket and got up to the podium and talked about our life together as kids, how we had always been there for each other, how he'd always say, "It'll be all right, Patty." I caught Greg's eyes when I said that. We both knew how hard it must have been for Steve to assure his sister that everything would be okay when we could look at our lives now and know that they never were.

After the memorial, Greg and I found ourselves back at my patio.

"You know you're still wearing his baseball cap?" Greg nodded in my direction.

"I know," I said. "I'm not ready to take it off."

He took a long swallow of beer. "You guys were always close," he said.

We sat quietly after that. I felt like I barely knew my brother, and at the same time, I knew him incredibly well. It was profound.

"You know, Patty, I'm not ready to go home. I don't want to go back," he told me.

Greg wasn't able to run his business in Hawaii any longer. He had been hearing voices in his head regularly and thought he should see a psychiatrist again. He wanted to stay with me.

I told him he could stay in the garage with Rocky, who was happy to share his space. He told me he'd help out around the house, get a job, and chip in for rent.

"It's going to be okay," I assured him. "It's going to be good."

Greg took my car to pick up some Chinese food for dinner, and I went to my bedroom. As soon as I opened the door, there were Stephanie and Buzz, high. Having Greg back in my life gave me the strength to finally say what I needed to say.

"Stephanie, I need to talk to you in private," I said without thinking twice.

As soon as Buzz left, I spoke as gently as I could. "Stephanie, you have to move out. Today."

"What do you mean?" she asked.

"I mean I can't do this anymore," I told her.

I told her I knew she had been taking things from me and that she was using and so was Buzz.

Stephanie stared at me for a long time. I didn't look away, didn't even squirm. Stephanie sighed, stood, and yanked her two suitcases off the closet shelf.

"Don't worry," she said. "I'm only taking what's mine."

Eventually, her suitcases were packed and she and Buzz were standing by the front door. Stephanie's eyes were wet.

"I love you, girlfriend," she said. "You know that, right?"

My mind was blank. I knew I should say something, tell her I loved her too—we had been friends for thirty years—but I didn't feel like saying it. I just wanted her to leave; I wanted this to be over. I nodded and closed the door behind them.

* * *

I'd done what I had to do when it came to Stephanie and Buzz. But it was like another death; things were changing so fast. Could I handle all the stress without a drink?

Sugar helped. I craved it constantly. As soon as I woke up in the morning, I would plan my "little party." I would go to the store and buy ice cream, candy bars, cake, and pie. I was getting fat fast. Now, six months after my last drink, I wanted and craved sugar all the time. Sugar felt like love to me; I was addicted. I could never have enough of what I didn't want—I didn't *want* cookies and I didn't *want* brownies, but because they felt like love, I gave in. I would sneak sugar, lie about eating it, hide it. I thought that if people found out I was eating so much, I wouldn't be worthy of their love, of connection. I thought I wasn't enough.

I tried practically every diet out there, but I'd lose five pounds, then gain six. I had no idea what to do. If I was triggered—whether it was from stress about money or worrying that I wasn't a good mother or frustration with Michael—I would stuff my feelings down and reach for something sweet to numb the pain. In that moment, I would lose my freedom. I didn't have the freedom to do anything else but get my sugar fix. I didn't have the freedom to say no. I was only focused on getting more; I couldn't think of anything else. I was ashamed of myself.

One afternoon, while watching TV and having my little party, I saw a woman on a talk show who was a psychic and spiritual medium. Her name was Sylvia Browne. I couldn't get enough of what she had to say. After seeing that show, I wasn't so sure that I was an atheist anymore.

The next day, I went out and bought Sylvia Browne's book and a few of her videos. And though I couldn't afford to get a psychic reading from her, I started getting readings every three months from her son, Chris Dufresne.

I was curious about my future and interested in understanding my past. He confirmed that Stephanie had been using heroin in my house for a long time and that she had been taking things from me. Getting accurate information about Stephanie and my past proved to me that someone or something beyond us existed, and I was ready to explore the possibilities. I was ready to change.

The first change I was ready to make was with my eating. I had heard about Overeaters Anonymous, and I decided to give the meetings a try. OA was similar to Alcoholics Anonymous. They followed the same twelve steps; they just replaced the word *alcohol* with the word *food* or *sugar*. I hadn't been interested in a twelve-step program before because I'd never believed in God or a higher power, which was what these recovery programs relied on. Now I thought OA might do me some good.

From the moment I walked through the doors of my first OA meeting, I knew I was home. A woman spoke about her struggle with food and sugar, and I felt like she was telling my story. For the first time, I understood that I wasn't the only one who had little parties.

Hearing about everyone's struggles with eating helped take my shame away. I started to understand that I was addicted to not only alcohol but also sugar. I learned about trigger foods. Any food containing sugar was a trigger food. Triggers started my craving for more, and for me, "more" meant eating candy or ice cream or cookies until I was stuffed.

After three weeks of attending weekly meetings, I chose a sponsor and met with him a couple of times a week. The first time we talked, he encouraged me to take some time at home to get down on my knees and ask God, or my higher power, any questions.

Alone in my bedroom that night, I got down on my knees and said out loud exactly what I was feeling. I said that I hadn't believed in anything before, and I asked if there really was a God or a higher power listening to me. If there was, I asked, would that God or higher power please let me know?

Simply asking the question opened my heart. I immediately felt a connection to what I have since learned to call God or Source or Universe. I felt a deep sense of reverence, and, for the first time in my life, I believed in something greater than myself.

What a start to a sober life. I lost a lot that year—my brother, my best friend—but what I gained was immense. I went to OA meetings every week, and though I struggled with a sugar addiction for years, I finally discovered a way not to feel ashamed when I slipped. The important part was that I believed I could make responsible choices, and when I slipped, I dug deep to find the strength I knew I had, then got back up and tried again. Each time I tried, I gained strength, and that led me to become empowered. I knew it was just a matter of time until I got to where I was going as long as I didn't give up—all the strength I gained from trying gave me the power to succeed.

Though I was still working as a prostitute, I started to consider the possibility of doing another kind of work someday, and even thinking about that felt empowering. Most importantly, I'd proven to my family and to myself that I could stay sober, and my kids were proud of me and were happy that they had their mother back. And on top of it all, I started on my spiritual path. A path that would lead me to amazing places.

Chapter Eighteen
The General

"**G**ood morning, General!" I said every day on the patio. "Good morning, Captain!" Greg always said back.

Greg lived with us now, and it was like a dream come true; he and Rocky had especially become very close. The kids called him U.G. (for "Uncle Greg"), and I called him the General. The General and I sat in my private patio as often as we could.

One day, I told him why I wore a pager. I told him about the cocaine, the alcohol, how I'd lost my home and my marriage. I told him how my car had broken down and how I had no money to fix it. He understood.

"Life gives us experiences that show us how strong we really are," he told me.

The truth was out in the open, and my brother had no judgments.

My brother was a spiritual man. For twenty years, he had been going to a spiritual center called Sukyo Mahikari. Sukyo Mahikari is a practice of experiencing spiritual energy as a universal life force. *Sukyo* means "universal principles," and *mahikari* means "light energy." Light energy is used for healing stuck energy or illness in the body.

As soon as he discovered a Sukyo Mahikari dojo in our area, Greg put down the bottle and started going every day. I had never seen my brother so happy. He gave and received healings at the dojo, and sometimes he stayed all day to listen to dharma talks on different subjects. He offered his skills as an electrician to people he met. And he always had good stories to tell about being there. Once, he said a woman came in with a burn on her hand and he healed her by holding his hands over it. The burn healed in front of his eyes. It was fascinating to hear about but hard to imagine.

Eventually, I became too curious to stay away. One day, I went to the dojo with him. And I loved it from the moment I entered the building.

We were called into a small room where people lay quietly on mats on the floor. Others knelt beside each person and held their hands a few inches over them, scanning energy fields for hot spots—trapped energy from accumulated stress or physical illness. When the healers found those places, they hovered over it, directing the healing light from their hands.

Greg and I lay down on our mats. A man dressed in a cozy-looking sweater and Levi's came over and knelt at my feet. I closed my eyes as he scanned my body. Now and then, a chant would begin, words I had heard my brother recite before. The chants were mesmerizing, and tears streamed down my cheeks. There was no emotion, either happiness or sadness—just pure release. After my session was over, I felt a deep sense of calm and peace.

I couldn't wait to come back. I went with Greg to the dojo as often as I could.

One day on our way home from the center, Greg told me about Transcendental Meditation.

"You can't believe how you feel," he told me. "Twenty minutes and you feel like you just took a nap for days." He told me about something called "the dive," where you go deep down into yourself, into your core, where it's quiet and calm.

"You've never felt that kind of peace, man," he said.

"I feel pretty peaceful at the center," I told him.

"You feel it twice as much with TM," he said. "Trust me."

He told me he'd take me with him when the time was right.

* * *

Three months later, Greg was drinking again. He stopped going to the center. It was sad to see, but I understood. My brother was so different when he drank. He already smoked over a pack a day, but when he drank, he smoked even more, and he had a hacking cough I knew was from smoking.

I was worried about him. I took him to the Social Security office to apply for Social Security Disability Insurance, with the hopes that with his PTSD, he could get some government money. He qualified, and he not only received a pretty hefty monthly SSDI check, he was now able to see a psychiatrist on a regular basis and get the medication he needed.

Six months later, he was doing much better. It made me happy.

One morning, I walked out to the patio and greeted him with the usual salute.

"Good morning, General!" I said.

"Good morning, Captain! I'm happy to tell you today that you've been a great captain. You deserve another stripe," he said. "You have orders to report to the TM headquarters next Monday. You're going to sign up."

He put his hand in his pocket, pulled out a wad of cash, and pressed it into my hand. "This is to tell you how much I appreciate you helping me," he said.

They were hundred-dollar bills, and there were ten of them.

"Oh my God! Are you sure?" I exclaimed.

He assured me he had plenty now, and he wanted me to have some. I threw my arms around him.

The next week, Greg took me to a Buddhist temple for a TM orientation meeting. I learned that the program involved a simple technique you practice for twenty minutes in the morning and twenty minutes at night. You sit comfortably with your eyes closed and repeat a mantra, which in this practice is a sound without meaning.

I repeated my mantra softly over and over to myself. In minutes, I felt a sense in my body I could only describe as diving deep, just like Greg had told me about. My mind was quiet. There were no busy thoughts racing around in it—no worries, no imaginings, no regrets. It was blissful.

At home, I moved my favorite chair into the corner of my bedroom to use as my place to meditate. Every morning and afternoon I meditated, and before I knew it, the days of practice turned into years of practice. How grateful I was to my brother for showing me something that changed how I felt every day. And I was grateful to myself for choosing to be sober so I could feel this good.

I never could have guessed where all of this would lead.

* * *

On my forty-eighth birthday, Dawn gave me a very special present. It was an audiocassette I'd mentioned to her about something called *self-talk*. I'd heard good things about it, but I had no idea that the tape would turn out to be one of the greatest gifts I've ever been given.

My self-esteem had always been very low. I thought I had common sense, but I didn't think I was smart. Everyone seemed to know so much more than me. Within hours of listening to the tape, I learned that I had worked hard my whole life convincing myself I wasn't smart and that it might actually not be true.

Self-talk was powerful. It shaped my beliefs and my behavior. My negative beliefs about myself came from my own self-talk. I could just as easily feed myself positive information about myself instead. With positive beliefs about myself, positive definitions of myself could become true.

I started by trying to say three words out loud: "I am smart." It was hard to voice the words, and it was harder to have to repeat them over and over, like the tape instructed me to do. I felt like I was lying. But after fifteen minutes of repeating them, it became easier to say them. The tape had prepared me for this; it was referred to as "blocking," or resistance. I took a deep breath and kept going.

For a couple of weeks, I played the tape every day, practicing the affirmations like mantras. I played it every time I was in the car, repeating the affirmations out loud:

I am smart.

I am good.

I am loving.

I am loved.

I am kind.

Before long, I was feeling better about myself. I not only believed what I was saying, but I was getting into the habit of naturally saying the most wonderful things to myself every day.

* * *

Four years into my sobriety, I got a call from Carla, who'd been a close friend for years. She needed a room to rent and wondered if I knew of anything.

Carla was like family. When the kids were little, we would go out on her boat and the kids got to go waterskiing. I thought it would be perfect to have a friend in the house because she could help with the rent and, even though Rocky had just turned eighteen, there would be another adult at home while I stayed at Michael's. I was so happy it could be Carla. And Michael was thrilled. He wanted me with him as much as possible.

"It's kind of an unusual arrangement," I told her, "but I have a place if you're willing to share a room with my brother."

Most of my personal belongings were already at Michael's, so I moved the rest out and I gave Greg and Carla my bedroom. Greg graciously gave Carla the bed and made himself a place to sleep on the floor. But soon they started sharing the bed. And in a few weeks, they were romantically involved.

My brother was in love. There was a lightness I'd never seen in him before, though he still drank and smoked a lot. His medication kept his illness under control, TM kept him balanced, and being in love put a spring in his step.

Within the year, Greg and Carla got engaged and moved north to live on a farm in a house close to Carla's daughter's house. Carla's mother had been diagnosed with terminal cancer, and she had come from Holland to live out the rest of her days with her daughter and granddaughter. Carla and Greg decided to wait to marry until after Carla's mother passed.

About four years later, I got the call. Carla and Greg were simultaneously making burial arrangements and marriage plans.

Eleven days after, the phone rang again. Through sobs, Carla told me she'd heard Greg coughing hard in the bathroom that morning. It wasn't unusual; he coughed like that every day. But this time, when the coughing stopped, Carla went to the bathroom to check on him and found him collapsed on the floor. She called an ambulance, but it was too late. Greg died of a heart attack at fifty-nine years old, on February 10, 2004.

I was in shock. The last attachment to my family of origin was gone. I was sad I would never get to see him smoke a cigarette again. As strange as it sounds, he seemed at peace when he slowly inhaled, then slowly exhaled, then looked up toward the sky.

Grief hit me hard after losing Greg. It seemed like we'd had so little time together, and it had all gone so fast. And yet in that short amount of time we had, he had given me the gift of a lifetime—TM. Transcendental Meditation was the foundation that shaped my spiritual life.

To this day, my brother is my guardian angel. And whenever I walk into my office, I look at his photo and give him the same greeting I would give him on our patio—I raise my hand to my head and say, "I salute you, General."

Greg's death was a huge loss to us all. But as the reality of it sank in, through my sadness, I felt gratitude. The last few years with Greg were so precious. I thanked God for my chance to have that relationship with my older brother, for us being able to help each other like we did and feel our love and acceptance. We really got each other. I may have wished him better health in his lifetime, but when I looked at what he had at the end, I could only be happy for him. He had love. He had hope. He had family.

He was, and will always be, the General.

Chapter Nineteen
Purple Ribbon

One day I was out shopping when I noticed a cute little glass vase. I examined it and thought, *I could make a pretty candleholder out of this*. I would put some potpourri at the bottom and a votive candle on top. It would be fun, and maybe it could even bring in some money. I ended up buying a dozen vases, a dozen votive candles, and a few big bags of potpourri.

Before I left the store that day, I also noticed some beautiful hollowed-out books. They looked like regular books, only they had no pages. Instead, there was an empty compartment to fill with whatever my imagination could come up with. I had no idea what I would do with them, but I liked the designs. They were surprisingly inexpensive, so I bought every book in stock.

Michael had an office at home he wasn't using, and he agreed to let me use it for my new business. I called it "Patty Sue's Crafts"—I knew Michael would love the name. My kids got on board, even with everything they had going on in their young-adult lives. Dawn was very supportive. Rocky created my logo, and Popeye helped me get a patent and a business license.

Every night while Michael slept, I went into my office, lit a candle, played soft music, and spent hours making my candleholders. I was in heaven. I loved pretending I was the CEO of a big business. I bought boxes and colored tissue paper and put everything together. I was ready for my first sales.

I called everyone I knew. People in the bingo room at our hotel in Vegas bought some candleholders. Even my dentist bought a candleholder. And for Mother's Day, Dawn presented me with a gift that she said all of her friends were giving their mothers that year—it was one of my candleholders. We burst out laughing.

My confidence had grown bigger than it had ever been, and I wanted more. On her TV show, Oprah talked about gratitude and how writing down five things you're grateful for each day sets you up to receive what comes to you. She explained that living life in a constant state of wanting makes it hard for the Universe to respond generously. Living in a state of gratitude gives the Universe an invitation.

I was ready to give it a try. I bought a new journal and called it my gratitude journal. Every day I wrote down five things I felt grateful for. I couldn't believe how much I had.

My gratitude journal made me wonder what else I could journal about that could be of help to me. I remembered Oprah talking about truth-telling. Every time we lie, she said, we give away some of our power. When we tell the truth, we give up the feeling that we should be anything other than who we are, and we gain power. My entire life had been filled with lies. I was curious to see how telling the truth could change it.

I started a truth journal, and every day, I wrote the truth about different things I had done in my life. It was hard, but I reminded myself that I told the truth now and that it was good to do it. I was encouraged by the proof I had from everything else I was doing— facing the hard stuff was way better than running away.

Inspired, I added a third journal, a courage journal. I wanted to face my fears instead of avoiding them. I started by asking myself what I was really afraid of, and I wrote it down. Next, I wrote down what I thought it would take to silence those fears. Then I wrote down five qualities I had that could help me overcome any obstacle. I wouldn't even have known I had those qualities before. Now I could name them and believe in them.

Whenever I did something that took courage, no matter how small it was, I wrote it down in my courage journal. If I stood up for myself, I wrote it down. If I said no without feeling guilty, I wrote it down. Starting with the small things and gradually moving to bigger things, I listed what I would change in my life if I could, knowing I had the courage to do anything I truly wanted.

Journaling every day on these topics had a huge impact on me, and that's what led to my big aha moment—I wanted to take it to the next level and spread the practice of this kind of journaling to others.

I created three types of journals—Gratitude, Truth, and Courage. I had them made at a printer and had the words beautifully printed on the covers. And then I put them inside the colorful hollow books I had bought without knowing why. Night after night, with my candle lit and music playing, I decorated the journals using fabric and a glue gun.

When I ran out of hollow books, I bought purple boxes and tied them with purple ribbon. Suddenly, I was struck with doubt about the ribbon. Was it good enough? Pretty enough? Did I choose the right color? I asked a few friends for their opinions, but then I remembered—I already had all the answers I needed. If I thought it was beautiful, wasn't that all that mattered? Even though it was just purple ribbon, this was a huge moment for me: for the very first time, I trusted my own opinion; I trusted myself. From then on, as other decisions had to be made, I didn't feel the need to ask anyone for the answers anymore. I realized that the only approval I'd ever need was my own.

One day, a mailer arrived in my mailbox from a local school. It offered free testing to anyone who was curious to know what kind of work they were best suited for. "Do you have the right job?" it asked. "Do you know what you're really good at? Call us for a free test to find out."

I'd always ignored mailers like this—I never believed I was smart enough for a career-style job. But for once, I was interested in giving the test a try. I wanted a job I could tell my children about and feel proud of.

The next week, I went to the school and took the test. The test said I was a humanitarian. I'd be best suited for a job in the medical field.

"I'm not the doctor or nurse type," I told the woman at the testing center. "I don't want to be in school that long."

"There are a lot of positions in the medical field," she assured me.

For years I'd seen commercials on TV advertising a career as a medical assistant. It looked somewhat appealing, but I never thought I would do anything about it.

The woman told me that two schools in the area offered free classes for medical-assistant certificates. I could have a certificate in less than a year, and all I had to do was buy my books. I decided I would sign up at one of the schools the next morning.

When I left the testing center, I had butterflies in my stomach, but I didn't care if I was fifty years old and the oldest person in the room. I wondered if I could I pull off my craft business and keep up with my studies at the same time.

* * *

On the first day of school, I felt a rush of excitement. I wasn't resisting "real" work anymore. It felt so good.

In line at registration, I made friends with a man who was registering for classes in the same program as me. His name was Jose, and he was trying to turn his life around too. He told me he had been a heroin user but that he was sober now. I shared a little about myself, and we were buddies right away. We took a few classes together, and I picked him up and gave him rides to school. We had classes in medical terminology, anatomy, physiology, lab, drawing blood and giving injections, and EKG and blood pressure. In the car, we talked all the way to school about what we were learning.

I worked for hours every day studying for exams, and it paid off—I passed all of my classes. On graduation day at the end of the nine-month program, Jose and I were proud.

The day after graduation, I scoured the classifieds for jobs for medical assistants. The first ad I responded to was for a job at a dermatologist's office. I landed an interview the next day and was hired on the spot. I would work three days a week, and I couldn't wait to start.

That office referred to all of their medical assistants as nurses, and I was the nurse for the coolest doctor in the office, Dr. Bonnie Kerr. I loved working for Dr. Kerr. I also loved Terri, the nurse who showed me the ropes.

I was using my brain and getting paid for it, and I loved every minute of it. I hardly ever had my pager with me anymore. I could finally say I was done with the prostitution business and mean it. There was only one man I would still see, the man from the glass shop thirteen years earlier. I continued to see him once a week, for the next four years.

＊

Not long after I started working for the dermatologist, Rocky came in to see the doctor for a bad case of poison ivy. I felt so proud. He finally got to see me in a professional setting, and, like it or not, Rocky was the lucky one to get my first shot ever—right in his butt.

Everyone at work knew I was engaged, but Terri and a few other nurses liked to tease me about it. They didn't believe Michael would ever marry me. We had been engaged for six and a half years. I always insisted that we just didn't have a date set.

In truth, I still couldn't bring myself to ask Michael to set a date, because I was still afraid of rejection. I just wore my cubic zirconia and believed it would happen one day.

Despite all of that, working a regular job was doing wonders for how I felt about myself. And the way I felt about myself improved even more the day one of our patients mentioned that she had been journaling. I told her about my journals.

"I have a boutique!" she said. "You should bring them into to my shop. I'd be happy to sell them for you."

I thanked her and promised I'd be there. It felt like everything was in perfect alignment.

＊

One day while meditating, I kept seeing myself telling my story to a large audience. This happened for months until finally I asked the Universe, "Why does this keep happening?" Immediately, a message floated in that said, "You're going to write a book that tells your story."

Really? I thought. *Wow.* It made perfect sense to me, and I would realize later that this would be my calling, my divine duty—somehow, I knew it would benefit others. I trusted it immediately, and that very day I bought a journal and began writing everything I did each day, trusting that the process would unfold perfectly and I would be guided.

And then, one day while writing, I just felt different. I couldn't put my finger on it, but then the words flew out of my mouth: "I'm not going to have sex anymore if I'm not having pleasure."

I had been faking pleasure all fifty years of my life, and I didn't have another fake in me.

As soon as I said that, my life began to change.

Chapter Twenty

Joy

I shared my epiphany with my new friend Kysha. Kysha was a psychic who I started going to spiritual events with. I knew she would understand. And she more than understood; she couldn't be happier to hear it. In celebration, she invited me to an event. She wouldn't tell me what it was.

"Trust me, Patty. You're going to like it," she told me.

I always liked the events she took me to, so I was fine with not knowing what it was. I was ready for something new, and I loved surprises.

Kysha and I arrived at a private home in the San Fernando Valley. I was introduced to a couple dressed in ceremonial Indian gowns. With a welcoming smile, the woman ushered us inside, where she smudged us with sage to clear our energy fields so we could enter the room without carrying any energy from outside.

We entered a large living room, where a man named Shri Param Eswaran sat on a large gilded pillow dressed in a Punjabi suit. About twenty people sat cross-legged on the floor facing him. Right away, I noticed one couple among them, a very distinguished-looking man and a gorgeous blonde. They were radiant. I could feel their love for each other across the room, and I knew right away, in that moment, that that was what I wanted in my life. I was ready for that kind of love.

Shri Param Eswaran spoke, using words like *Shakti* and *Shiva*, *lingam* and *yoni*. I had never heard these words before. We sat quietly watching as a fully dressed woman lay down on the floor with her knees bent and a man knelt in front of her, leaning forward to chant "om" into her vulva.

"Oh! Is this event about sex?" I blurted out, without thinking. I heard a few murmurs of "yes" from around the room.

I had no idea what this was all about, and it wasn't like anything I'd ever seen before. The couple was doing something that looked sexual but that wasn't sex. It seemed to be about the woman's pleasure, about energizing her genital area, or, what I learned they were calling by its Sanskrit name, her yoni. The blonde woman smiled at me from across the room, and we caught eyes.

I couldn't believe it! The Universe had heard me loud and clear. I wanted more from sex, and here everyone seemed interested in learning how to deepen their sexual experience, combine love with sexual pleasure, and recognize its spiritual and sacred qualities. It was more than I could have ever imagined.

We were asked to pair up with someone we hadn't met and sit cross-legged, face-to-face. I paired up with the man seated next to me. We were told not to speak or even introduce ourselves, just to gaze into each other's eyes and see who was there.

I felt like I could see this man as a little boy; I could see a playfulness in his eyes. I noticed an expression that looked like fear, or hope, or some kind of uncertainty. I smiled at him, hoping to help him feel more relaxed with me, and then I realized smiling was almost like talking, so I stopped smiling and tried to be more neutral. It was all so complicated. *Just gaze*, I reminded myself. Was it my own vulnerability I was feeling? Was I trying to take care of him to resist letting myself be seen?

Shri Param asked the group to face him again and chant "om"

together. I heard a woman near me sniffling, but I kept my eyes closed and my chanting steady. I could see how someone could feel emotional from this. I couldn't have been happier.

When the event was done for the night, Kysha wanted to talk with some friends of hers, so I went into the kitchen and got in line for some food. I felt a tap on my shoulder and turned to find myself looking into the face of the beautiful blonde woman. She opened her arms wide to embrace me.

"I'm Joy Mitchell," she said.

I introduced myself, and she asked if I would come and join her. I couldn't think of anything better.

"You seem happy," she said, smiling her brilliant smile.

"I am so happy," I said. "I had no idea where my friend was taking me tonight, but I'm so glad I came."

I told her about my decision to stop faking pleasure with sex.

"I've never had pleasure with another person in my entire life, and I'm fifty years old," I shared. I figured if I was going to tell anyone, she was the person, and tonight was the night to do it.

"Well, you've come to the right place, haven't you?" she said.

Joy told me about her new book, *Love Ever After: How My Husband Became My Spirit Guide.* Through channeled conversations she had with her deceased husband every day for two years, she learned what she needed to know to write the book. The book came, in effect, from the other side. With his guidance, she wrote about a twelve-step program to manifest dreams. One of her dreams was to have love in her life again after her husband's passing. Only six weeks after she followed the twelve-step program, she met the next love of her life, the man she had come there with that night, Jerry.

Jerry was fifty years old, and Joy was seventy. I couldn't believe it. She looked so young and had so much energy.

"And believe me," she said, "sex gets even better with age."

"Sexy at Seventy," an article Joy wrote about her sex life, was published in *Our Turn, Our Time*, a collection of essays by women over fifty about what they find most fulfilling in the second half of their lives. It let women know it's never too late to have a great sex life.

The rest of the evening was beyond wonderful. Joy and I traded phone numbers and made plans to meet for lunch.

When we met at a café the next week, Joy told me more about herself. For more than fifty years she had dedicated herself to helping others find their own paths of joy. Besides being a writer, she was also an astrologer, teacher, hypnotherapist, and minister. She was the first woman to ever have a cable television show on astrology. She had read horoscopes for thousands of people and had taught and lectured at schools, charities, and civic organizations. Subsequently, she held the position of vice president and chief astrologer of XII Signs, publisher of the monthly Starscrolls found in supermarkets and vending machines around the world. She had written several books, including the one she had told me about the previous week, one of them about love and astrology.

She told me about her kids—she had three, like me. Her son, Elliot Anders, was an Emmy-nominated composer, and her daughter, Terri Nunn, was the lead singer of the band Berlin, who won an Academy Award in 1986 for "Take My Breath Away," from the movie *Top Gun*. Her stepson, Bruce Lisker, was wrongly convicted of murdering his mother and spent twenty-six years in prison.* Phone calls with Joy helped keep him going.

Joy and I spoke openly. When she said, "If you're not living on the edge, you're taking up too much space," I knew our attitudes about life were in alignment.

---

* He was exonerated in 2009.

"I totally agree," I said. "If your dreams don't scare you, they're not big enough."

Joy nodded and said, "I'll drink to that." We toasted with our iced teas and laughed.

I felt so comfortable with her, and I wanted to go deeper and share about the choices I'd made in life. I told her about my marriage and divorce and about the prostitution. She understood completely. We also talked about my crafts business and my new job as a medical assistant. My life was changing now that I was starting to focus more on myself and what I wanted, I told her. Joy offered me an astrological reading and said that all she needed for it was my date, time, and location of birth.

The next day over lunch, Joy told me I was going to become an expert at something new and that I would attract a lot of people. I couldn't wait to know more.

I took Joy's reading to my psychic, a well-known channel named Pepper Lewis, who channels Gaia, or Mother Earth.

Pepper told me I would resolve the difficulty I have with expression in my throat area. I would also create a process that would first lead to my own healing, and then I would teach it to others and I'd even write a book about it. As always, I left Pepper's reading feeling excited and optimistic about my future. Change was ahead, and I was right on track, heading into it.

Michael knew nothing about any of this. He would never understand or even be interested, so I didn't share it with him. I stopped faking pleasure when we had sex, but Michael never said a word. At that point, I didn't really care. I was focusing more on me now. Still, I wasn't ready to end our relationship or stop going to Vegas with him. I was loyal to him, and I was longing to be wanted. I wanted to know

I was good enough, that I was marriageable. I didn't even know what that meant; I just wanted it.

During the drives to Vegas and by the hotel pool, I read books. I especially loved Joy's book *Love Ever After*; it opened me up to a deeper understanding of life and life beyond.

Michael made it easy. I didn't have to explain anything to him about what I was reading, and I didn't need to understand anything more quickly so I could tell him about it. The quiet time was good for keeping my mind off how unfulfilled I was.

And the real light of my life was my new and amazing friend. Joy and I would go to lunch and talk about everything. I thought that maybe soon I would attract my soul mate, just like she had. First, though, I had to understand the soul—my soul—better.

I went to the tantra workshops that she and Jerry recommended, and I met the local tantra community—men and women around my age who had come with the same sort of desire I had for depth in love and sex. These were spiritual people, people interested in communication and connection, just like me.

What happened next was exactly what Joy and Pepper Lewis saw in their readings: I was about to get behind the wheel, my transportation to my destination.

Chapter Twenty-One
The Driver's Seat

I hadn't driven on a freeway in twenty-three years. That made it pretty hard to get around LA, the city of freeways.

Not long before I'd met Joy, Kysha and I were going to an event. On the way, she wanted to stop by her friend Effay's house to drop something off. He lived forty-five minutes away. Kysha had lost her driver's license, so I had to drive.

"We'll have to head out early," I told her. "You know I don't take freeways."

Kysha frowned. "We can't take city streets! It'll take an hour and a half!"

"Sorry," I said. "It's the only way I can go."

We pulled up to the house over an hour late. The moment Effay opened the door, I started to explain. "It's my fault," I blurted out. "I don't drive freeways."

Effay was an older man, trim and almost bald, with kind, dark eyes. He was a therapist, and he also worked in the film business. Kysha had told me he had MS, which was why he used a cane. He smiled a big, warm smile and motioned for us to come in.

"You don't drive freeways?" Effay asked.

"It's not that I've never driven freeways," I told him.

"You don't drive them," said Kysha.

"No, I don't," I said. "But I used to. I drove them all the time."

"Why did you stop driving them?" he asked.

"One time I had a panic attack while driving the freeway, and I haven't driven them since," I said.

"I might be able to help you, if you're willing to try," he said.

"This guy's good, Patty," Kysha chimed in. "If anyone can help you, he can."

I considered it for a moment. No one had ever offered to help me before.

"We'll get you back on the freeway faster than you can imagine," he said.

All week long, I thought about how inconvenient it had been to not be able to drive the freeways all these years. I was so neurotic. If someone was going to drive on the freeway while I was in the car, I needed to know exactly how long we'd be gone. I counted the minutes until I was home again.

There had been so many times I couldn't take the kids to the beach because the trip took so long. Sometimes we would have to stop on the way because I was having a panic attack and we'd have to stay at a motel and then drive the rest of the way home the next morning.

I didn't like asking for rides. In the days when I drank, I had to drink a six-pack just to be a passenger.

It took me almost two hours on city streets to get to my first meeting with Effay.

Effay asked me to tell him about my first panic attack on the freeway. I told him about following Bert in the rain.

"Is it possible you didn't want to follow Bert, period? Freeway or no freeway?" he asked.

I thought for a moment. "I probably had some doubts," I said.

Effay explained chakras to me, the energy centers in our bodies. I had never heard of chakras, but I was ready to try whatever might help.

He had me lie down on the couch. He coached me through breathing, relaxing, and letting my tension melt away. He took me through the seven major chakras, starting with a red light at the base chakra and moving upward by color—orange, yellow, green, blue, indigo, and white. He had me envision a white light entering the top of my head and filling my body. Then I envisioned it forming a protective shield.

As I sat up slowly, gazing at him through my blissful fog, he handed me a cassette tape. "Take this, and do it at home," he said. "It'll help you, trust me."

I thanked him and made another appointment for the following week. I listened to the tape every day. It guided me in balancing my chakras, just like I'd done in my sessions with Effay. And right away, I could feel a change taking place within me; I felt calm and centered. When my chakras were open, my energy could run through them freely, and harmony existed between my physical body, mind, and sprit.

One day, Effay asked if it was time—if I was willing to take back my power.

I had to laugh. "Do I have to do it on the freeway?" I asked.

"When you're ready," said Effay, calm as ever.

He told me to get a tape recorder and a headset before the big day so I could record the name of each off-ramp as I came to it.

"It'll give you a sense of control," he said.

The next Friday, we met at 5:00 a.m. so I could practice before there was traffic.

"Ready?" he asked.

"Ready," I answered.

We drove the dark city streets, following signs to the freeway, and my heart pounded hard. The light turned red at the corner before the on-ramp, and I took the time to do a mini chakra balancing. I briefly visualized each chakra, starting at the base and moving upward through each color. It only took a minute, but I felt balanced and centered. Then I put on the headset and turned the tape recorder on. The light turned green.

"When you're ready," said Effay, "put your foot on the gas pedal and drive up the on-ramp and onto the freeway."

My throat felt thick and I couldn't speak, so I nodded. I drove onto the on-ramp.

"Now, just say what you're doing," he said.

"Here I am going up the on-ramp," I said.

The on-ramp ended in a merge lane, and thankfully there were no cars. I put on the left turn signal.

"Here I am entering the freeway," I said. I sailed into the slow lane, picking up speed.

The sky was still dark, and the freeway was practically mine. Effay was right. Narrating each moment gave me something to think about besides being scared. I called out the name of the first exit.

A few cars passed in the fast lane, nowhere near me. I called out two more exits. At the fourth exit, I told Effay I was done. I was feeling anxious.

Effay had me exit and do another mini balancing.

I got back on the freeway and made it past four more exits. And then I exited, took another short break, and got back on the freeway and headed home.

I did everything Effay suggested, and all of it worked.

"If you're up to it, I think we should go out again tomorrow morning," he told me.

"I can't say I'm excited," I said, "but in a way, I can't wait."

We had a few more early morning sessions together, and then I was ready to go it alone by driving home on the freeway after our session. I did a mini balancing and put my headset on. I drove off, imagining Effay cheering me on.

I went straight to the freeway and merged with the rush-hour traffic, only exiting once for a mini balancing before getting back on. I called Effay the second I got home.

I did it. I was in the driver's seat at last.

Except with Michael. He wasn't going to change just because I was. The caregiver in me saw that Michael needed me now more than ever, and although I had always wanted him to need me, there was a shift. I needed myself.

My eyes were opening, and I was beginning to see that I had a choice—I could be there for him at the end, or not. With his body starting to break down from all the drinking, the doctor said his system was wearing out and that he should quit. But he wasn't having any of that. Either way, I needed to take care of myself.

Three mornings a week, I worked for Dr. Kerr, and in the afternoons, while Michael went to the North Woods, I went to Joy's. Joy had macular degeneration, and her eyesight was getting worse. She couldn't drive anymore. She asked me to be her personal assistant, running errands with her and answering her emails. It was a great incentive to get on the freeway and drive the forty minutes from the San Gabriel Valley to the San Fernando Valley.

Joy was amazing. When she became legally blind, she started practicing strengthening her channeling abilities. She decided to bring her community to her and share herself and her psychic abilities. She started holding monthly gatherings that she called "Sundays of Joy." About twenty of Joy's good friends would gather in the rec room of her condo. For an hour, she answered pressing questions people had about their lives and their futures. She told me she wouldn't trade this inner vision for her eyesight again if she had the chance.

Before we met, Joy had started another powerful gathering called "Goddess Camp." The camp was a place where eleven women—all of them handpicked by Joy—gathered for a long weekend four times a year for self-empowerment. I wasn't invited to go to the camp when I first learned about it as it was full and closed, but many of the women who came to the Sundays of Joy went there, and whenever it was someone's birthday, they sang a special birthday song.

One of the most unforgettable moments of my life came that spring, on my birthday. At lunch after the Sunday of Joy, to my surprise, everyone sang to me:

Happy birthday! Happy, happy birthday,
We are proud of you! And we love you!
May happiness be yours, through all the coming years,
And all the best to you! And all the best to you!
So keep on smiling every day, and let your troubles melt away,
And may you never, ever, ever be blue. Oh, Patty!
Happy birthday! Happy, happy birthday to you! Wonderful you!

I had never felt anything like it before. I had friends. I had community.

I didn't know it then, but in just a few short years, I would become a Goddess too, replacing Joy when she became too ill to attend. The Goddess Camp became pivotal in my life, just like Joy herself.

Meanwhile, Michael was getting sicker and sicker.

Chapter Twenty-Two
The Marrying Kind

"If you stop drinking, you might live another year or so. If you don't stop, expect another few months," the doctor told Michael.

"Guess I'll have to try some of her root beer tonight," Michael joked. The doctor didn't seem to think it was funny.

Michael's skin was sallow. His eyes looked gauzy, his pace was slower than ever, and he was relying on his scooter and cane all the time now.

Michael had one glass of root beer at the North Woods that night. And then he chased it with a beer.

After the doctor's news about his health, Michael wanted to go to Vegas more often and stay longer. He was tired of hurrying home so I could get back to work. He told me he wanted more time with me—the magic words.

I had worked at Dr. Kerr's for almost two years, and I couldn't imagine leaving. Though I'd been giving Michael half of my paycheck every month (he never asked me to pay for anything, but I wanted to feel like I was doing my part), I liked having a paycheck. It was a thrill every time I opened the envelope.

I felt sorry for Michael. He didn't have any real friends, and the only time he ever saw his daughter was Christmastime. I ended up giving my two-week notice at Dr. Kerr's. I was sad to leave. I questioned if I was doing the right thing, but habits are hard to break. Sometimes it takes a few lessons before we get it.

Soon enough, I was putting the wants and needs of a man before my own. But the difference this time was in my awareness—I recognized that I had done this in every relationship I had ever been in. I stuffed my thoughts down out of fear—the fear that I wouldn't say what he wanted to hear. I was so afraid to upset him or to appear bossy. I thought my power would be unattractive. I just wanted to be perfect. It worked—he was proud of me and paid attention to me.

Life with Michael quickly became about going to Vegas for ten days every few weeks. The Golden Nugget was our second home. I spent most of my time meditating twice a day and reading my books by the pool. Michael hung out at the bars.

At home with Michael, I was always available to him. I did his pedicures. I wallpapered his house. I ran his errands. In the mornings, I gave him the sexual pleasure he wanted. I went with him to the North Woods and nursed Diet Cokes while he drank more than ever. I was trying to be what he wanted, in the hopes that I would be enough. In the hopes that he would marry me.

Finally, I hit a wall. I was sick and tired of never questioning why we had been engaged for over eight years with no wedding plans. Why we had never once talked about it. I knew his health wasn't great, but I didn't care.

One morning in bed, I snuggled up to him and put my head on his shoulder. "Michael, when are we getting married?" I asked, as casually as I could.

A long silence followed. A long, painful silence.

Eventually, he spoke. "You know I'm not the marrying kind."

His words hit me like a sledgehammer. I started to cry. Hard. I felt a pain I'd never felt before. It was like an avalanche of sadness sliding down a mountain, and it sliced my heart wide open.

While I sobbed into his shoulder, he didn't move, didn't say a word. Then, to my even greater shock, without opening his eyes, he asked, "Will you suck my dick?"

My stomach lurched. How could he say that? Was this all I was worth to him? I was paralyzed. And then, still crying, I moved downward under the sheets. Through my tears, I tried to pleasure him. I felt I deserved this level of a relationship. After all, I had been selling my body for sex these past fifteen years, and although I was finished doing that (or nearly finished—I still saw my client from the glass shop), I could now see that Michael was using me in the same ways all those guys had. It felt dirty.

Then, finally—finally—I couldn't go on. I threw back the sheets, climbed out of bed, backed away, and took a good look at him. He just lay there with his eyes closed, his expression totally blank.

And that's when I could finally see. He was unavailable and always had been. I was done trying to win his love. He wasn't "the marrying kind"? What the hell was the marrying kind? Someone who knew how to love? He was right. He wasn't that person.

Deep, deep down, I'd always known I was a trinket on his arm. I knew he wasn't the marrying kind, but the fear of acknowledging that paralyzed me. If I dared to think the thought, then I'd have to do something about it, and I had no idea what that would be. All those years I refused to see how he was stringing me along. I knew it, but I was afraid to admit it to myself. I didn't know another way to get the love I craved, and I didn't even know what it was.

I'd been on autopilot, but I'd finally found the courage and strength to break out of my lifelong habit.

I took off my engagement ring, set it on the nightstand, and walked out of the room.

I sat down at the kitchen table to cry my heart out. And then I called Joy and Jerry.

An hour later, I was on their doorstep. They took one look at my swollen eyes and folded me into their arms right there in the foyer. They held me and rocked me while I cried some more.

"You have enslaved yourself, sweetheart, and now you have set yourself free," Joy told me. "Never forget this moment."

It was hard to hear those words—*enslaved yourself*—but I knew she was right.

I wanted to rent a room somewhere, but I didn't have enough money. I needed to sell the Cadillac Seville he'd bought me. I'd get another job and support myself.

Though I still had a lease at Club 2nd, all the rooms were occupied, and I didn't want to move back in. I'd start fresh somewhere new, somewhere special and all mine.

I went back to Michael's later that day and acted like nothing was wrong. As it would turn out, walking out on Michael wasn't easy. The feeling of being unwanted, unloved, and alone still tore at me.

At lunch a few days later, I told Joy what was going on.

"It looks like you've got more layers to heal," she said.

"I've had my heart set on marrying him one day," I told her. "It's a lot to give up."

Joy wasn't convinced I was interested in actually being married to Michael. She thought I was interested in the idea of being married to Michael.

"Let me tell you something," she said, looking straight into my eyes. "If you leave this jerk, he will want to marry you."

"That sounds pretty backward," I said.

"Trust me," she insisted.

I did trust her. Completely.

For the next two weeks, I kept my distance from Michael, while brownies, cookies, and ice cream helped numb my pain. It was still too hard for me to talk about, the rejection hurt so much. I started to create a plan. Michael planned to go to Vegas at the end of the month. I would tell him I couldn't go with him, that there was a wedding shower I wanted to attend. He'd never ask about a wedding shower or want to go. I would say I wanted to hire a house cleaner while he was gone so it was sparkling clean for him when he got back, and I would ask him to leave me a signed check to pay her. In truth, she would help me pack and load a moving van.

As soon as Michael left for Vegas, all went according to plan— until I opened the glove compartment of the Cadillac to get the car registration. The car was registered in Michael's deceased wife's name. The car was another one of his "gifts" to me, just like the fur coat, that was never supposed to leave his house. I slammed the glove compartment closed and said, "Fuck it! This was supposed to be *my* car, so I'm going to keep driving it anyway, and he'll have to deal with it."

I was enraged. I called Joy.

"You ask why I'm never mad about anything, and you know I don't swear much, but I'll tell you something, I'm *fucking mad* now!" I shouted. It was Joy who got me thinking about the fact that I had never gotten mad. And now I wanted to show her that I could tap into this anger. It felt more intellectual than physical, but it was as mad as I could get.

"So it took losing everything for you to get angry. It's good you're angry. Good things can happen when you're in touch with your feelings," she said.

I knew she was right. And I was done stuffing my feelings down out of fear that Michael would reject me. I mustered up all the courage I could and decided to turn this crisis into an adventure.

Since I couldn't sell the car, I decided to cash the check he gave me to rent a room. It was my only option. I made sure to make it an amount that wouldn't cause the bank to call Michael to approve it. I decided on $7,500.

That amount seemed completely fair to me. I had given up my job to be his caregiver, his unpaid caregiver. And for what? Plus I had given him half my paycheck every month for eight years!

The bank teller knew me and Michael, and she cashed the check without question. I was on my way.

When I drove away from Michael's that day, the feeling I felt most was freedom—pure, beautiful freedom. I wasn't afraid anymore, and I loved where I was heading. Even if I had no idea where that was.

Chapter Twenty-Three
New Life

I drove to Sierra Madre and parked in front of the first coffee shop I saw. I bought a newspaper and looked through the classifieds over lunch. I circled any rental that looked good.

Luck was with me. The first listing I called turned out to be the one.

Before dark, I signed a rental agreement for a lovely, completely furnished room in a big house on a quiet street in Sierra Madre. It had French doors that opened to a private rooftop deck and a kitchen downstairs that I shared with the landlady—a widowed retired schoolteacher. I couldn't have been happier.

A month later, I had a job working as a medical assistant for a doctor in Culver City. Unfortunately, he was nothing like Dr. Kerr. He saw at least forty cancer patients a day, and it was far too fast-paced for me. I hated it from day one.

But life was good. I loved my quiet room. It was my sanctuary, my freedom place. I went to sleep every night relieved to finally be free of being stuck in Michael's manipulations. Surprisingly, he hadn't tried to contact me.

And then I started dating a man named Barry.

Barry was an actor and singer-songwriter around my age. He was a spiritual man, which I loved about him. He liked hiking, so we hiked the Pasadena foothills together.

One day while having lunch with Joy and Jerry, they asked how my sex life was going.

"Not very well and still no pleasure," I said. I told them it was hard to ask for what I wanted.

"If you get a whip, it will help you feel powerful, so you can ask for what you want," Jerry advised.

So I got a whip. Barry was as surprised as I was when he saw it in my hand. With the whip in my hand, I was able to ask for what I wanted.

"Stroke the small of my back gently with your cheek," I told him.

Just saying those words helped me feel a sense of power I hadn't felt before. It opened me to using my imagination, and I found it arousing. And yet it did nothing for Barry.

Our lack of chemistry and inability to get on the same page helped me see that we weren't compatible. I had spent all those years chasing the wrong dragon with Michael, and I wasn't about to do that again. I didn't want to waste any more of his time or mine. So we broke up.

* * *

The day after Christmas that year, Rocky called. He was nineteen years old, it was nearly the dawning of a new millennium, and he was having a party to usher in the New Year. He invited me to come, and I said yes. Then Rocky broke the news: "Dad's coming. He's going to be the bartender," he said.

I did my best to sound like it would be the most natural thing in the world to be at a party with Bert.

"That's fine," I said. "I don't mind."

Bert was a good man who was trying to do better. I knew we'd both played a part in our failed marriage, and I wasn't resentful. I was so different now; I had a new life. I was part of a community, being mindful each day, coming into myself, and moving toward wholeness. I was in a good place. So maybe seeing Bert would be a good thing too.

Rocky was about to start a new life too. He was moving in with a friend and was waiting tables at a local restaurant. At this point in time, the General had moved in with Carla, and the tenant renting the studio was gone. Popeye and his girlfriend had rented a house nearby, and Dawn lived close to her college, with a roommate. So after almost eight years, I was going to return the key to the landlord and say goodbye to Club 2nd. I couldn't wait, but I was also sad. The kids had basically grown up at Club 2nd.

Before the party, I took the time to meditate. I thought about how I'd seen the kids' friends grow up all those years at Club 2nd. Some of them would be at the party. Some had never even known me sober.

When I arrived at the party, the band was playing and the house was packed. The kids greeted me with hugs and good wishes as I made my way to the dining room. Right away, I saw Bert, waving hello from behind a busy bar. I walked up and said hello. He came out from behind the bar and gave me a hug. He looked good.

"You look beautiful," he said.

I asked for a Schweppes on ice with a twist of lime. He poured me a glass and handed it to me with a grin, his eyes sparkling.

"Busy lately? I hear you're working," he flirted.

"Busier than ever," I shot back.

"We should go out sometime," he said. "I mean, if you can get some time for me."

I still cared about Bert, but I had no intention of starting up with him again.

Not long after we brought in the New Year with shouts and hugs and kisses, I bid farewell to Bert, said goodnight to Rocky, and got in my car to drive home. As I backed out of the driveway, I said goodbye to Club 2nd and all the insanity that had been part of my life there. I felt grateful that through it all, we still had love.

* * *

Early in the New Year, Michael surprised me with a phone call. He didn't ask me why I'd left. He didn't even ask me how I was doing.

"The house should have been cleaner for seventy-five hundred dollars," he said.

"I had no choice, Michael," I told him. I tried to sound cool and collected, but my stomach turned at the sound of his voice. "I couldn't sell your dead wife's car, could I? You know, your gift to me?" I could hardly believe I had said that out loud. It felt so good.

"I think I might just have to tell the bank what you did," he said. He sounded slimier than I remembered.

I asked him not to do that, ignoring the voice inside of me that warned, *Look out. He's got power over you when you're afraid.*

"Come down to the North Woods tonight, and we'll talk about it. You've got my car. You can drive over here." He hung up.

I didn't want him to call the bank. So I went to the North Woods right after dinner.

Over his beer and my iced tea, Michael explained several confusing reasons why he needed to put the car in Madame Queen's name. And then he made me an offer, a trade—he wouldn't report my taking the money if I helped him out at home. His refrigerator was empty, his house needed cleaning, and his list of errands was piling up.

I held back my laughter. The manipulator. He was doing whatever he could to get what he wanted. He couldn't ask me outright for help. He couldn't say, "I miss you," or "Will you come over and keep me company?"

Thank God I never married him. He didn't want me, the person I was. He wanted me to be his companion, his housekeeper, and his caregiver. He wanted me for sex.

I saw it clearly now. But I didn't want to be in trouble with the law. So I agreed to his terms. I would go to his house every week to do his laundry, grocery shop, pick up his prescriptions, and, once in a while, cook him meals.

"But I am not staying over," I told him, "and there won't be any sex."

He didn't miss a beat. "You can leave my car here the next time you come over."

The next morning, I called my client from the glass shop and asked if he knew of anyone selling a used car.

"As a matter of fact," he said, "I have a car I want to get rid of. I'll give you a good price."

Chapter Twenty-Four
No

Effay gave me an anthology of women's sexual fantasies to read at home. I felt nothing.

Then he showed me 35mm films taken of real people making love—not porn, not actors, no one drunk or on drugs. I was astounded.

Up until this point, I had only seen a few porn films, but they were a turnoff and were hard to watch. There was nothing loving about them. All they did was support my belief that my only worth, my only value, was my body and that giving away my body right away was the only way to feel like I was enough, the only way men would love me.

But in these films, the couples were affectionate. The women weren't faking it. I could see it was real.

The women didn't avoid being touched, and they weren't trying to get it over with. The men were tender, interested, and making eye contact. Conscious touching. Real pleasure.

Up until this point, I thought men only wanted their own needs met. I was amazed to see how they genuinely loved pleasuring the women and how much enjoyment that gave them.

Watching these films was a game changer for me. I realized I couldn't fake it and feel pleasure at the same time. I had no idea what true intimacy was, but I was ready to find out.

My turning point came with a book called *For Yourself: The Fulfillment of Female Sexuality* by a sex therapist named Lonnie Barbach. I read every single page and learned how to get to know my body and to get comfortable with pleasuring myself.

It worked. After six weeks of reading the book and doing everything Lonnie suggested, I discovered that I wasn't broken at all. I could feel sexual pleasure.

My first spiritual sexual experience was an intense pleasure that I got to gift to myself. Recognizing that I was the one in charge of my own pleasure, I let the intensity keep building and building until I finally burst into an orgasm that went on and on and on, so long that I could not doubt what I was feeling. Sobs of the purest joy and love poured from the core of my being and pulsed in every cell of my body. A clear vision of a body map appeared in my mind's eye. It was my body, with electrical currents running between my nipples, clitoris, and vagina, up to my brain, and out to the tips of my fingers and toes. I was connected to myself—alive, sexual, and radiant. I was a beautiful human being, complete and perfect. For the first time, I felt at peace with my sexuality.

One day, I was talking with Reverend Paul and his wife at the Science of Mind Church. He and I had become friends, often talking after his weekly class on spirituality. I shared with them about the breakthrough I made by reading Lonnie Barbach's book. I told them about how I was learning to receive pleasure for the first time in my life and that it was making a huge difference.

"Hearing about this from you could benefit a lot of women in the community," said Reverend Paul. "What would you think about putting some material together and leading a class?"

Wow! I finally had something to offer. I was sure I could help other women. If I could receive pleasure, any woman could.

That night, I stayed up until three in the morning creating a class based on *For Yourself*. But at a board meeting the next week, it turned out that not everyone thought the church was ready for my workshop. Some people were afraid my class would cause the pews to empty out and that no one would ever say why they were leaving the church. So I quietly retreated from that venue.

But I was on fire, and my old friend Bill Lipton could see that. He introduced me to one of his coworkers at the Brain Institute, and it was decided: I was going to teach a class for women.

I started teaching a six-week sexual anatomy class to help women get familiar and comfortable with their bodies. The purpose of my class was to empower women and help them enjoy their sexuality. I shared my story with the ten women in the class, who were married and unmarried and between the ages of thirty and sixty. Two had been prostitutes who said they felt safe to share with me, which thrilled me.

After that, Bill invited me to speak at the Conscious Living Foundation, a spiritual center he had created. And another reverend at the Science of Mind Church offered me her home as a location for more classes. It was indescribably rewarding to make a difference in even just a few lives.

Joy was extremely proud of me, and I was pretty proud of myself too. I had no idea where this was leading, but I had a feeling it was leading somewhere good.

And then Michael called.

"I've been getting things in order so we can get married," he said. "That's what you want, right?" *What?* I thought. *Am I hearing this right?*

I remembered Joy's words: *If you leave him, he will want to marry you.* I had completely given up on the idea of marrying Michael.

But I said yes anyway. I shocked myself with my answer. I thought I had let it go. I thought I had moved on.

The next day, Michael called and asked me to meet him at his lawyer's office. He instructed his lawyer to draw up a prenuptial agreement. He had promised his house to his daughter when he died, but I could live in the house for up to five years, and I would receive five thousand dollars, but that was it. It felt strange, like we were making a business deal, and he was the boss.

Numbly, I started to plan the wedding. It was happening the following Friday. I wasn't even excited. Not one bit. There was no one I wanted to tell about it, no one I wanted to invite. But I found a preacher and secured a location anyway.

Two days before the wedding, Michael called and asked me to stop by the North Woods. I sat across from him at his table, uneasy. His eyes filled with a lustful, devilish look.

"I wanted to remind you to pack some of those sexy little nightgowns for our honeymoon," he told me.

My stomach flipped. The look in his eyes was horrifying. This was the man who would be my husband in two days? He looked like a dirty old man. What was I doing? I jumped up and started toward the door.

"I'll see you at the house," I called over my shoulder. I shuddered and ran to my car.

"I cannot marry him," I said out loud. "He makes me sick!"

All these years, I'd been so caught up in wanting love and attention from Michael. I had been obsessed with thinking that marrying him would prove he loved me. But what would it really mean for him to love me? I'd never thought about it. I never really looked at the man, never asked myself if he was someone I wanted to marry. I had avoided believing the truth of who he was: unavailable. It wasn't his fault. He was who he was; he hadn't changed. It was I who had woken up. And just in the nick of time.

I drove to his house to wait for him. He didn't act surprised to see me sitting at his kitchen table.

"Michael. I'm not marrying you. I can't," I announced.

He barely looked at me. "I'm sorry you feel that way."

And that's all he said. He disappeared into the bedroom for his afternoon nap.

I let out a deep sigh as I heard his bedroom door close. I'd done it. I'd finally taken myself back.

* * *

A few months later, Michael called again. He started by asking how I was doing, something he never usually did. I knew he wanted something.

"I'm doing great," I told him.

"Are you happy?" he asked.

I told him I was happy, that life was good. Except for my job. I hated my job.

Never one to miss a chance to make a deal, Michael made an offer.

"Look," he said. "You're miserable at your job; I'm miserable at home. Come back and live with me and be my caregiver. I'll pay you."

Pay me? That was new. I told him I had to think about it.

The next day, I called him back and said that I would do it—I hated my job that much—and I gave him my terms: weekly paydays and my own room to sleep in, in exchange for housekeeping and errands as needed, and no sex. He agreed. I quit my job the next day and gave my landlady a thirty-day notice.

At Michael's, I painted and wallpapered Michael's daughter's old room. I filled the closet with my clothes, set up a meditation area, and put my treadmill in front of the TV. This was my new space.

One night, Michael tapped at my door.

"Patty Sue, will you come to bed with me tonight?" he asked.

"Absolutely not," I told him, with no hesitation.

It was quiet.

"If you don't, I'll fire you," he said.

"Then go ahead and fire me!" I shouted.

He walked away.

By saying no to him that night, I was instantly empowered in a way I'd never felt before. I felt amazing and proud. Powerful and strong. I was finally at a place where I truly loved myself. No matter what.

And now that I had finally found my *no*, I knew that when I did find my *yes*, it would be real.

Chapter Twenty-Five
Captain Corelli's Mandolin

There was nothing I could do to help Michael. He drank like nothing mattered. And he started acting strangely.

One day at breakfast, he cut and ate his toast with a knife and fork, like it was normal. I had never seen him do it before.

Sometimes, he didn't finish fastening his pants. I caught him several times leaving for the North Woods that way.

A week later while getting dressed, he fell back onto the bed and slid to the floor. I heard the crash and called 911. At the hospital emergency room, the doctor examined and released him and told me he was drinking too much and it would be better if he stopped, "even now." I knew it was never going to happen. I thanked them kindly.

For the next few days, I insisted on driving Michael to the North Woods and staying there with him. He wasn't sure where to sit; he didn't recognize the bartenders. He would forget his briefcase was next to him on the seat even though it had been part of his daily ritual for years. One day, he was so confused he started driving his electric scooter in circles around the parking lot instead of steering it toward the entrance. I called 911 and had him admitted to a hospital.

I stayed in his hospital room for four days to keep him company. I always knew I would be there for him when he died, and I felt it would be soon. Who else did he have?

I called Michael's daughter to let her know. She thanked me for telling her, and that was it. Nothing else. She never visited him, never called.

When the doctor released Michael to go home on hospice, I ordered a hospital bed to be set up in his office. When he asked for a beer, I gave him a cold bottle of Miller. He didn't drink any of it. I figured he wanted the feel of a beer in his hand, like he usually had as we watched football on TV.

Over the last eight and a half years, I'd wanted to open this broken man's heart, and it never happened. Now he was paying me to take care of him, and he was dying at home, with me as his caregiver.

The hospice nurse would check his vitals and administer morphine, then step into another room. While Michael and I were alone, he started saying things like, "Who are all these people?" But there was no one in the room except me. I sat at his bedside knowing I was about to witness this man's transition home, where he could rest in peace.

Sitting at his deathbed, I thought about what I'd learned from the spiritual teachings of Abraham-Hicks—that there is no separation between what is physical and what is not, that there isn't even a lapse in consciousness. "Death" is a matter of closing one's eyes in this dimension and literally opening one's eyes in the other dimension. And the reemergence into Source Energy is always a delightful thing.

When Michael breathed his last breath, my thoughts were of forgiveness. I had no anger or resentment toward him for anything, and there were no tears.

I was grateful the hospice nurse was there to help me with calls to the coroner and funeral home. It was nine days before Christmas of 2001.

Not long after, with Michael gone and the house empty, I went

out to see a movie. I saw *Captain Corelli's Mandolin*, starring Nicolas
Cage. Completely unexpectedly, I cried my heart out. But I wasn't
crying over the movie; I was crying over my unfulfilled dreams with
Michael.

I went back to see that movie three days in a row, each time crying
hard and long. I planned to go every day until I had no tears left.

On the fourth day, there were no more tears. I was complete.

* * *

I planned a small memorial for Michael at the North Woods with
Michael's daughter, her family, and my three kids. We ate lunch at a
long table and talked about Michael and his life. A glass of beer was
placed at Michael's empty seat in his honor. Michael had been the
North Woods' most devoted customer since the day the place opened.
Except for when he was in Vegas, for thirty years, Michael had been
seated at his table every day at 11:30 a.m.

I found it eerie being alone at Michael's the night of the memorial, almost lonely. Michael had been my steadiest companion and
biggest frustration for a long time. What would happen now?

The next day, Michael's daughter called. She thanked me for
caring for her dad. Then she told me that I had to find another place
to live. She had inherited her parents' house and would be renting it
out. I could stay six months, but that was it. I didn't say a word. She
went on to tell me that she was executor of her father's estate and
would be handling the financial matters. Which was another way of
saying I had nothing to do with anything related to Michael anymore.

Seven years earlier, when we were first engaged, Michael told me
he'd put $85,000 in the bank for me as an engagement present.

"This is for you. But you can't have the money until after I die,"
he told me.

Near the end, he told me, "You don't have to worry about a thing."

I thought he meant he had put me in his will. But I didn't ask, and he didn't say.

Later that day, I went to the bank to check on the account, and the teller told me the account was closed. Michael had closed it only two months earlier, while I was living with him and working for him.

I called my friend Kysha. Since Kysha was a psychic, I had a feeling she'd have some information for me.

We sat at Michael's kitchen table, and after a few moments in silence, Kysha got up and walked to the grandfather clock in the entrance hall.

"Patty!" she shouted. "Come here! Do you see what I see?"

I went over to look at what she had found—toward the back, from a certain angle, I could see papers were concealed beneath a black towel at the bottom of the clock. I tried to open the clock case, but it was locked. I had no idea where the key was. The only way to find out what was in there was to break the glass.

I found a hammer and a roll of duct tape to tape the glass. I hit the glass three times with the hammer, breaking it enough to safely reach in.

Underneath the towel was almost three thousand dollars in silver bars, coins, and stacks of two-dollar bills he used for tips in Las Vegas. There was also the passbook showing that Michael withdrew $85,000 when he closed the account.

I gasped. I had broken off our engagement, so I didn't expect the engagement money, but it hurt to know he would hide every cent. That he didn't tell me about the grandfather clock. That he took the exact amount—$85,000—out of the bank account. He had been sneaky until the end. It made sense that this manipulative man was once a pimp. He still acted like one. And now I was left alone to look at my choices, because this was the man I had chosen to stand by until his dying day.

Kysha went into the living room and sat at the baby grand piano. Suddenly I was hearing the ragtime music I recognized from the North Woods. I followed her into the living room and sat down on the couch, shocked by what was happening. When she finished, she looked up, like a trance had broken.

"I've never played ragtime music before. I don't even know how to play it!" she exclaimed.

I couldn't believe it. She'd played the song like she had played it a hundred times before. Michael listened to that music every day at the North Woods, and his energy was obviously in the room with us. It was strange to watch Kysha channel Michael but also fascinating.

Michael's house was a fine holding place for the next six months while I figured out what I wanted to do next. I understood his daughter. She was who she was, and I knew the apple didn't fall far from the tree. I was happy to move on.

I didn't feel much of anything toward Michael after crying my heart out at the movies three days in a row. Even after all those years, in truth, I didn't miss him, and I wasn't going to miss the house. Club 2nd had always felt like my home; his place never had, ever. I was looking forward to a new life.

* * *

Before long, I took a job as a live-in caregiver for two men with mental disabilities. I prepared their meals using food that was delivered by a government agency. I helped them pick out what they would wear for the day and helped them to their buses for their day care programs. It gave me a little income, but I didn't like the job, and I knew I couldn't take it for very long.

I called my good friend and former sister-in-law, Diana, in West Covina. I might have divorced Bert, but I had never divorced the family. Diana offered me a room in her house for as long as I needed, and I was able to help her through an emotionally difficult time as well. Since my path had converged with Joy's, I felt comfortable guiding her and offering spiritual practices that would help her heal. Through her husband's connections with management at Trader Joe's, I got a job there and quit working for the men with disabilities.

I still spent time with Joy three times a week, going to her house to help her answer emails, help her with errands, pick up groceries, and eat lunch at her favorite restaurants. Her vision was deteriorating fast, and we both cherished the time we shared.

Through an online dating service, I started dating a man named Martin. Martin was a talker, which bothered me a bit, but I reminded myself that you get what you ask for. And I had asked for this—after Michael, I was starved for meaningful conversation.

When I told Martin I was interested in learning more about tantra, he said he was curious, and we agreed to go to a workshop together. We went to a tantra workshop with Charles and Caroline Muir. After the workshop, I decided immediately that I wanted to teach tantra someday. I wanted to share what I had experienced so that I could help women learn to feel and help couples be conscious in relating intimately with their partners and understand the partnership beyond the traditional sexual connection—deep eye gazing, breathing together in sync, recognizing each other as equals with no hierarchy. I had no idea how it would happen; I just knew I wanted it.

Diana was feeling much better, and I had saved enough money to get a place of my own. When I told Martin, he asked if I would move in with him. I had my reservations; we'd only dated for a few months, and I wasn't sure it was a good idea, but Martin was insistent.

Once again, I didn't listen to my intuition and agreed to move in. Right away, I knew I had made a big mistake. It was hard living with Martin because his incessant talking was wearing me out.

Joy taught me an important lesson: be careful what you ask for, and be specific! I was a powerful woman, and the Universe was listening. Which meant that if I could be specific about what I wanted, I could have it.

And soon, I would.

Chapter Twenty-Six
John

I t was spring of 2004, and Joy and Jerry invited me and Martin to a tantra workshop. Maybe tantra was what Martin and I needed, I thought. Maybe we could finally get somewhere in our relationship. I was unfulfilled, as usual.

In truth, I didn't like him. I was acting like I liked him in hopes that I would. He wasn't interesting, and he talked way too much. I'd known from the moment I met him that I wasn't attracted to him. But I was desperate. My longing for love was so strong that it allowed me to turn a blind eye. So I agreed to go to the workshop.

The workshop was at the Hustler store in Hollywood and was led by a man named John Tierney and his partner, Shama. Next to shelves of sex toys and racks of G-strings, John and Shama spoke about heart, spirit, breath, sound, and movement.

Afterward, Joy brought John over to our table. I liked him right away. He seemed kind, confident, and humble. We talked about me and Martin possibly doing private tantra sessions with him and Shama. Martin, as usual, took over, talking way too much. Everyone backed out of the conversation, and then we all said goodbye. Driving home that evening, I knew for certain I was in the wrong relationship—again.

Yet I still took Martin with me to see Shama for a session, in an attempt to learn how to have more intimacy together. Alas, it didn't work. Martin just couldn't go there.

I hadn't been ready to end it before, but I was ready to end it now. And I was ready to do it quickly and cleanly—I didn't hang on, try to make it work, or try to change him. I wasn't willing to waste any more time on a relationship that didn't feel good. Coincidentally, my relationship with Shama did feel good, and I eventually became her apprentice, helping her at tantra workshops.

I moved in with a woman named Jackie. Joy had introduced us several years before, and we'd become good friends. Jackie was a calming presence, a successful businesswoman. She had recently retired, owned a big house, and decided a roommate would make for good company. We were a good match.

For the next year and a half, I continued to explore my spirituality. I had worn a lot of masks and had taken off most of them. I was ready for authentic power. I continued to remind myself of the importance of setting intentions before making my next moves. I was done living unconsciously. For the first time in my life, I didn't need a man to love me, and I was comfortable being alone with myself. I loved it.

A few months after I moved in with Jackie, she told me about her elderly wheelchair-bound father-in-law, Syd. She asked if I was interested in living with him and looking after him. He had a beautiful house in the hills in Bel Air. I'd have my own room and a lot of quiet time, and he was a good man. I respected the elderly immensely and appreciated their wisdom and experience. Plus, a free place to live and a good job with good pay was something I couldn't pass up, so I accepted Jackie's offer with delight.

The year I spent with Syd was an honor. He was a sweet man most of the time, but on some days, for no apparent reason, he was stubborn or angry. As Syd's caregiver, I was guided by my heart and acted out of love. It felt good to be able to care for a man without needing him to like me. I cared for him with patience and compassion to the end.

When Syd passed away the following year, Joy helped me find the perfect studio apartment in Santa Monica, and I applied for a position at a caregiving agency. First Michael, then Syd, helped me to see that I was being led down a path, one that would be the foundation for my next career.

My first client through the agency was Mrs. Gately, who lived in a spectacular house on a hill in Bel Air with a view of a garden filled with rosebushes and a large pool with fountains. One quiet afternoon, we sat in front of that window for a cup of tea.

Mrs. Gately and I were as different as two people could be. She had been a world-famous opera singer and had lived a life of ease and privilege. At eighty years old, she carried herself like a queen. Two years before, she'd had a brain aneurysm and had been unconscious in the hospital for three months.

"The doctors said it was a miracle I lived," she told me.

Mrs. Gately's world was turned upside down. She had to relearn basically everything—how to walk, talk, eat, and write. She couldn't drive. She needed help every day.

"I lost so much of my independence," she explained with a sigh. "My life is completely colorless."

I reached out and put my hand on hers. "I'll give you the very best care possible, Mrs. Gately. You can count on it." Mrs. Gately was tearful, and I was grateful that I would be able to genuinely care for her. I knew I was a good person who cared about helping people.

I moved into the maid's room in Mrs. Gately's three-level home and provided live-in care four days a week. Monday through Thursday, I had a room where I could meditate and enjoy a view of the garden, and I had Mrs. Gately's wonderful company. Friday through Sunday, another caregiver took over, and I stayed at my apartment in Santa Monica and enjoyed my time off. I didn't mind the back and forth; it felt familiar.

One day, I told Mrs. Gately my story—all of it.

"I've never heard anyone tell the truth like you do," she said. "You've brought the world to me."

Things changed for me and Mrs. G in the summer of 2005. On one of my nights off, she fell and broke her hip, and, after the hospital, she went to a live-in rehab facility. I would still spend time with her as a companion, but for a few weeks, my hours were reduced to four half days per week, which meant I needed more work.

At Mrs. G's rehab, I noticed the people being discharged. I wondered who would help them when they got home. One day, I decided to ask these people about their post-rehab plans. For the most part, no one had any.

The next morning, I filed for a business license. I'd decided to officially open my first caregiving company: Patty's In-Home Care. I was so excited; I knew I could do this. When I was young, my mom never told me I couldn't do anything, and because of that, I believed I would succeed.

I had much to learn and much to do. Popeye gave me a laptop to use for the new business, and someone I knew who ran a caregiving agency showed me the ropes. On my time off, I handed out business cards and brochures at local rehab hospitals.

When Mrs. G came home from rehab, I went back to staying with her four days a week, and I was grateful to have the other three days to myself to develop my business. At last, I had found the right business for me.

Mrs. G told me she was very proud of me. For quite some time she hadn't been happy with the agency she was with, so she decided to quit using them, and she became one of my clients.

* * *

It was on a Friday in late summer of 2005 when I picked up Joy for lunch and found her more serious than I'd ever seen her. She climbed into the car and looked me straight in the eyes.

"Patty," she said, "my cancer's back. My time here will be shorter than I thought."

It couldn't be true. I reached for her, and we hugged tight.

"I was so angry the first day I heard it was back," she continued, "and then I connected with my guides. I've been reminded of how wonderful it is on the other side, Patty, and I can accept this. I know we'll all see each other again when the time is perfect." My eyes were so teared up I could barely see.

I had known this day would come, but I'd never wanted it to. Five years earlier, Joy had noticed a lump in her breast. At Jerry's insistence, she had it checked out and discovered it was cancerous. The next year, they were married, and after that, Joy had a mastectomy. She agreed to low-dose chemotherapy and avoided the test results. She just wanted to live the best life she could for as long as she could and not give energy to the disease.

"So I'm going to live my life to the fullest every day and do what makes me happy," she told me. "Now let's go have lunch."

Two weeks later, about thirty people gathered in Joy and Jerry's living room. Everyone had been told privately that Joy's cancer was back, but no one knew what she was going to say.

"I have an announcement to make," she said. "A very exciting announcement. I know there's a lot ahead, but I want to focus on our new workshop right now. Jerry and I want to take our big love bigger and help others find the relationship of their dreams. This will give me joy."

Joy and Jerry's workshop was called "Twelve Steps to Finding Your Soul Mate," and it was based on the program that had brought them together.

I was first in line to sign up. What if I could meet my soul mate? It was about time. I was ready.

The workshop was held a few weeks later. Joy explained to us that you could write down exactly what you wanted, ask the Universe for it, and then get out of your own way to receive it. You had to be specific, and you had to believe. I believed it was possible because I believed in Joy.

I went home and wrote my list of what I wanted in a partner. I wanted a man who liked to talk about ideas and things that interested me. Someone who was smart and caring. Someone who showed affection, someone who loved my children and could show it. I wanted a partner I could be intimate with and feel loved by and could share life-changing sexual pleasure with.

When I finished my list, I lit a candle on the altar and meditated. I thought about what I wanted, and I took it into my heart, consciously examining how it would feel to have a mate who truly loved me and cared for me and who genuinely liked me. I wanted to feel this way about him too.

I meditated on what I wanted and on belief in myself: *I am worthy of this good; I can have this good.* Then I let go. As Joy had told us to do, I opened myself to receiving what would come.

Two weeks later, I received an intriguing email from John Tierney. He and Shama had ended their relationship, and he wanted to get to know me better.

I knew John was polyamorous. Polyamory is a form of

nonmonogamy that involves emotionally and/or sexually intimate relationships with more than one partner. It usually involves a primary partner and an intimate relationship with one or more other partners. When practiced consciously, there is honest communication among all parties and there are agreements on boundaries.

I wasn't interested in polyamory. So I declined John's invitation and continued dating Ed, a guy I had just met on a dating site, though it turned out that Ed didn't seem to be the partner I ultimately wanted.

Later that year, I saw John at Joy and Jerry's Christmas party. There was an undeniable spark between us, but I was in no rush. I trusted that when and if something was right, it would happen.

In January, John called to invite me over to his place.

"We can visit, do some tantric massage," he said, "get to know each other better." This time, I was ready to see who he was. Without hesitating, I said yes.

It felt good to be with John. I loved his energy and found him very handsome, with beautiful green eyes and a warm smile.

I thought, *Here is another opportunity to find out who I am and be that person.* I was ready to be myself instead of the person I'd been up until now, the person I thought people wanted me to be. I was ready to speak my mind and be honest. I had been suppressing my thoughts and opinions for long enough. I was ready for freedom! For the first time, I cared more if I liked John than if he liked me.

With John, I felt my body relax in a way I had never experienced before. I wasn't anxious. I had no hopes or expectations. I simply enjoyed every moment of our time together as we sat on his living room floor getting to know each other and watching a recording of a Bee Gees concert on TV.

John's career was in the medical field, and when we met, he was a sales representative for Life Alert. I told him about my caregiving

business, but I wanted to take our conversation deeper, more intimate. I told John about some of my past. I knew I had to be honest if
we were really going to get to know each other and that it was better
to get it over with now than to wait until we were more involved.

"You know I've been a prostitute, right?" I asked casually.

"No," he said. "I didn't know that."

He didn't back away from me, shake his head, or show any reaction I could read. And I was surprised that he hadn't already heard
this about me from someone else.

"Really?" I asked. "I haven't kept it a secret."

John nodded, clear and calm. "It is surreal," he said. "It doesn't
seem like you."

I had to smile. "So how is it for you to know?" I asked.

He looked at me with no judgment. "You don't have any charge
about it, so I don't have any charge about it."

My heart soared. I had told my truth, and he was not shaken by it.

We talked about polyamory. John was finished with that, he said.
"I'm ready to be monogamous again. It's who I really am."

I looked deeply into his eyes, and I could see that I could believe
him. And I knew without question that it was more than me just
wanting to believe him. This was real. He was real. I was ready for
real.

And he taught tantra! And he gave me the most wonderful tantric massage, which uses sexual energy to achieve a higher state of
consciousness; there is no sexual stimulation involved. I felt opened
and awakened by his sensual touch and knew I wanted to explore
more of this kind of massage with him.

Before I left, John asked if I'd like to meet for lunch the next
Tuesday.

"I look forward to it," I told him.

* * *

It was cloudy on March 14, 2006, when we met at a small Italian restaurant in Santa Monica. We sat on the patio, where it began to sprinkle, but we didn't mind; it was sweet. I didn't tell John it was my birthday. I simply wanted to enjoy our time together.

We were getting closer, and the feelings were strong, with a sense of safety and ease like I'd never felt before. I wasn't "in love" like I had been with most of the other men I'd dated in the previous fifty years. I was more ready to love than I had ever been.

John was in his early sixties and told me he was an alcoholic and had quit drinking when he was forty-eight. I admired him for sharing with me so openly. That kind of intimacy was the best birthday gift I could have asked for. John told me about his childhood. He mentioned that he had been an altar boy, a choir boy, and a good student who had received a scholarship to a highly respected Catholic high school and then to a prestigious college. I told him I had been sober for nearly twelve years and had quit drinking at age forty-six. Instead of any judgment we could have feared from each other, there was even more that we could understand about each other. This prepared me for his more vulnerable, in-depth share that was to come.

After a few months when John felt safe with me, he told me that several years earlier he had uncovered memories of being sexually abused by a priest as a young teenager.

"As a result of the abuse, I no longer respected any authority figures. I wasn't going to be the respectful 'nice person' my parents and teachers expected me to be. I rejected anyone who espoused that behavior. I was no longer going to be the good boy everyone thought I was," he told me. "I was sick of doing the right thing. Subsequently, I thought that if I did all the things I was told not to do, my life would change for the better. In retrospect, I was subconsciously putting up a wall around myself so I would never be taken advantage of again."

After acknowledging this and learning about how it had shaped his life thus far, he began his lifelong healing journey. This was before the public revelations that uncovered the scope of the Catholic church's involvement. John knew there had to be many others who were experiencing the effects of abuse. He felt deeply about this. It wasn't long before he had started helping other survivors of abuse.

* * *

Now I knew for certain that I didn't want to date Ed anymore. I ended it quickly and cleanly, which was a big step for me. It felt great to make a choice like that so early in a relationship.

After a few months, because John felt safe with me, he told me he had recently uncovered memories of being sexually abused by a priest as a young teenager. It wasn't long before he started helping other survivors of abuse.

John and I went out every Friday night to an Italian restaurant called Capriccio's and had great, stimulating conversation. I loved his deep, caring nature.

Our first kiss was amazing. We had been dating for several months when our passion for each other led to an over-the-moon experience in the bedroom. For the first time in my life, I had gotten to know and love a man before becoming sexually involved. I was out of my head and into my heart. It was like being plugged into a circuit board. There wasn't even a chance of faking it. Every time we made love, it was better, which is what tantra does. I had never felt this kind of chemistry before. I was no longer caught up in the fantasy about love, and I knew the love I had for myself was real, so I didn't worry or have any fear that I would abandon myself. And because I was not going to abandon myself, I had no fear that someone else could.

For the first time, when I said, "I love you," it didn't mean, *Do you love me?* At last I had found my first real love. I knew I wanted to be with John for the rest of my life.

Six months later, on December 8, John proposed to me at Capriccio's. We felt pure joy, elation, and happiness.

Over lunch a few days later, I told Joy about our engagement, and she couldn't have been happier. "What a perfect place to have an intimate engagement dinner," she said. She and Jerry invited us back to Capriccio's to celebrate.

During dinner, John and I shared about our wedding and honeymoon plans. We spoke about true love and how grateful we all were to have found it. I told Joy that I was the luckiest woman in the world to have her in my life. I thanked her for opening a new world to me and teaching me so much. Joy told me that I was her biggest mirror and that she had never met anyone as positive as she was.

"You're even more positive than I am," she said. "You're the happiest person I've ever known."

"Wow, Joy. That's a lot to take in," I said.

Joy held me close. "Breathe it in. Just breathe it in, sweetheart."

It was a magical evening that we would never forget.

There was so much to do before the wedding day, and for the first time in my life, I was marrying a man I wanted to marry, not because I needed him to love me or because he needed me, but because we wanted to be with each other.

Chapter Twenty-Seven
Mother's Day

"**M**ake it your number one priority to feel good about yourself," Joy always said. And I did. And so did she. To her final breath. In March 2007 Joy sent out this letter to the community:

SUBJECT: "My Last Adventure"
Dear Friends,

Although I'd like to speak to each one of your personally this is not possible, so I'm writing this letter to let you know what's going on with me.

As most of you know I've been dealing with cancer for the past 6 years. Now I seem to be entering the last chapter of my life. On Feb. 15th I learned that the breast cancer has spread to my liver and that the loss of energy I'd been experiencing for the past few months is the result. From the very beginning I've chosen quality of life over quantity. And I am still making that choice. Chemo would only make me weaker and doesn't promise a cure. Since I am now 79 I feel that I've had a full and fabulous life. And I'm not afraid to die.

As an astrologer the timing of my transition was not a surprise to me. Also from my experiences talking to my

Guides and dozens of souls on the Other Side, I'm not fearful, angry, defeated or depressed.

After meeting with my doctor last month I experienced a great deal of sadness for the rest of the day and evening as I thought about everything I would be missing in the future. However, the next morning I awoke with an entirely different perspective.

My Guides assured me that "dying can be a great adventure"—and that's exactly what I intend to make it. So I am choosing to turn this last chapter into one of the best of my life. I intend to use my limited energy in positive ways rather than in fighting and resisting my condition by focusing my attention on trying to find miraculous cures and alternative healing possibilities. Of course I am open to "miracles" and feel they are more possible when I am vibrating joy, love, gratitude and acceptance rather than all the negative vibrations that come from fear and resistance. And that's where I'm coming from. I'm not TRYING to come from there, that's where I live . . . that's where I've always lived. Nothing has changed.

I've been a teacher most of my life and I view these last few years with cancer and blindness as a test to see if I could "walk my talk" in spite of these physical challenges. I've received enormous "gifts" from them which proves once again that EVERYTHING that happens is for our benefit.

Every teacher learns a great deal from their students and I'd like to thank you for all you've taught me. But I will continue learning throughout this last adventure. And beyond. As Yogananda stated—"Death is only an experience through which you are meant to learn a great lesson: you cannot die."

With My Love & Blessings,
Joy Mitchell

On Good Friday, 2007, Joy succumbed to cancer.

Joy not only modeled how to live; she modeled how to die. In her last days, she planned her celebration of life, a party that more than two hundred people attended in a beautiful garden in Los Angeles.

I learned so much from Joy. She taught me that we all have what we need to fulfill our dreams, and that if we can dream it, we can have it. She taught me that we all grow at our own pace in our own time and not anyone else's. She taught me that how we feel about ourselves is reflected back to us by our experiences, not another's experience of us. Because of Joy, I learned to follow my heart, choose what feels good to me, and let that be my guide. I don't need a situation or a particular person to make me happy. I can decide to be happy. Joy taught me that we are all worthy simply because we were born.

My grief felt bottomless. But I was grateful for the precious memories. And grateful for Goddess Camp. I was honored to take Joy's place after she was gone. The women there were the most magnificent mirrors, each of them committed to bringing their highest selves. For the first time in my life, I wasn't on the outside looking in. I was an integral part of a group. I truly belonged.

And on top of that, I was finally feeling real, mutual love with a man I respected, admired, and genuinely liked. For the first time in my life, I had gotten to know and love a man before becoming sexually involved with him. I had relaxed into being myself and saw John for who he was. We were best friends.

I married John Tierney on September 29, 2007. The wedding was held at a lovely private home in Sherman Oaks. As Joe Cocker's "You Are So Beautiful" played, my children and I walked across a wooden bridge over a koi pond. When John and I looked into each other's eyes, I knew our marriage would be eternal. To this day, he fulfills me as my spiritual partner, husband, and lover.

"Joy and I are passing the baton to Patty and John to continue the healing in our community and in the world," Jerry toasted at the reception.

John and I had a glorious honeymoon in Maui and Kauai.

I was living the life of my dreams, and my children were busy with their lives. Popeye owned a successful computer business. Dawn was building a life on the East Coast. Rocky began down the same path that I had, but instead of hiding from his problems, he decided to deal with them, head-on.

Not too long after John and I started dating, Rocky called me for help. He had been drinking alcohol, smoking pot, and using meth, ecstasy, Vicodin, Xanax, and OxyContin. Rocky was able to ask for help, and now I knew how to give it. I located a good twelve-step drug rehab called Warm Springs, and Rocky did the work to get sober. After rehab, he went to daily AA meetings, and Popeye started going with him—because Rocky had motivated Popeye to realize that he was an alcoholic too.

When I saw my boys quit drinking, I was inspired to start a path of healing for all of us. I knew I was going to publish my book at some point and share my story with the world. Until then, I decided I was ready to tell the truth, my truth, to my children and to listen to theirs.

If I could let go of my painful secret and speak the truth out loud—if I could tell them that I had supported my family for seventeen years as a prostitute—I could let go of the lies that kept a wedge between me and my children. We could have an authentic relationship. A mother's life goes on after her children are grown, and she has her own dreams to fulfill and her own gifts to bring to the world. It would be hard and it would take courage, and if I could do it, I would be the mother I had always wanted to be: honest and in my power. I remembered something I once heard: "No matter what you do, those who love you will love you, and those who don't, won't." I knew my kids loved me. But would they accept me?

It was almost Mother's Day, and Dawn was flying in from the East Coast so we could all be together. Rocky lived in Huntington Beach. And Popeye had a client near my house, which allowed us to meet for lunch once a week. It was easy for me to decide who to tell first; I would start with Popeye.

On the morning of our lunch visit, I paced in my living room. I'd decided to write out what I wanted to say to Popeye.

"Joy," I prayed, "please help me find the words."

I sat at my desk and took three deep breaths. And suddenly, I smelled gardenias. Joy had told us that she would come to us through the scent of gardenias. All of a sudden, I knew exactly what I needed to write. I started typing.

Just as I clicked the button to print, Popeye knocked at the door.

"Come in, sweetheart," I said. "It's good to see you. There's something I want to tell you before we eat."

"What's up?" he asked. "Is everything okay?"

Popeye followed me into the living room, and we took a seat on the couch. My heart pounded hard. I took a deep breath.

"I have to tell you something I've never told you before," I started. "I'm going to read you something I wrote. Then we can talk."

I held the pages out in front of me.

"This happened right after we moved to San Gabriel," I began, "right after your dad and I split up. You were nine." Then I read what I'd written.

When I was finished reading, I looked up at Popeye. He was staring at his hands in his lap.

"Are you telling me you never worked in real estate?" he asked.

"I was never a real estate hostess," I replied.

"Did Sam and Ted know what you were doing?" he asked.

"I told Sam about it," I said, softly. "I met Ted doing the work."

"Are you serious?"

"I am."

Popeye's eyes filled with tears. I'd never seen him so hurt. It broke my heart to be the cause.

"When parents lie to their children it's usually because they don't want to upset them," I said. "I still don't want to upset you, but I can't cover up the truth any longer. I want to be honest with you. I want you to trust me."

I imagined he was in shock. Ashamed of me. Angry at me. His mother. We sat in silence. Finally he said, "I guess we better eat lunch. I have to get back to work."

We ate quickly. Afterward, we gave each other a big hug. "I love you, sweetheart," I told him.

"I love you too, Mom," he said. And he was out the door.

"Promise you'll call if you want to ask me anything or say anything, okay?" I called out after him.

"Sure, Mom," he said, waving without turning around.

I did it. I felt relieved—and grateful to have been able to tell my truth to my son.

The very next day, with the same papers tucked into my purse, I drove to Huntington Beach to Rocky's apartment.

"I can tell you've got something on your mind," he said. "Good news, I hope."

I sat him down and read the pages straight through, and my

voice didn't shake. When I was finished, his eyes were wide, but he didn't frown. He didn't yell at me, and he didn't cry.

"Wow. That's something," he said.

"We can talk about it," I told him. "You can ask me anything."

"I don't have anything to ask about."

"Really? You don't have any questions?"

He shrugged. "What can I say? 'Why did you do it?' You just told me. I get it. You did what you had to do."

I got up and hugged him tight.

"It's okay, Mom," he said.

Rocky's reaction didn't really surprise me, but I was grateful for it nonetheless.

Later that day, driving along the Pacific Coast Highway, I rolled down the window to breathe in the salty air. Two of my kids knew now. There was only one left to tell, and she would be the hardest one.

My relationship with Dawn had been hard for a long time, ever since the night I drunkenly dumped the kitchen trash on her while she was sleeping. My shame had tied a tight knot around me. And deep down I was afraid, paralyzed by her words that next morning: "Don't touch me!"

I had thought that being sober and going back to school would help me be a mother my kids could love and be proud of. I thought that being a medical assistant and having a company of my own was what I needed to be the mother my daughter was craving. For the last ten years, my daughter had been very loving, but I still walked on eggshells around her, always afraid of rejection.

A few days before Mother's Day, I picked Dawn up at the airport and took her to lunch in Santa Monica. We were catching up on each other's lives, but I was distracted by thoughts of how and when to read her what I'd written.

After lunch, we started driving back to my house. At some point, I couldn't stand it any longer. A block before the freeway on-ramp, I quickly turned onto a residential side street and pulled over.

"What are you doing, Mom?" Dawn asked.

"Sweetheart, there's something I have to tell you," I said.

"Oh, no. You're scaring me!" She turned to the window. "I don't want to hear it, Mother, whatever it is."

"Dawn, I really have to tell you this," I insisted.

I opened my purse and pulled out the papers. I started reading, never stopping once to look up. When I finished, she turned to me.

"I cannot believe you just did that!" she shouted. "I told you not to tell me, and you went ahead and told me anyway!"

"I'm sorry, honey, but I had to tell you now. I had to tell you in person. I've told your brothers, and I wanted you to hear it from me," I said.

"You lied to me! What else don't I know?! Wait—don't tell me. Please don't tell me," she begged.

I took a deep breath and said, "I was never a real estate hostess."

Her eyes were slits now. She turned away from me again and covered her face with both hands as she burst into heart-wrenching sobs.

"I am so sorry to upset you, Dawn. I never wanted to hurt you. That's why I lied. But I can't lie anymore," I said.

She didn't say anything. I started the car. I recognized that in my need to tell her, I had crossed a boundary. And even though crossing her was the last thing I wanted to do, I also had to let my daughter know the truth. There was no turning back. We drove in silence the rest of the way to my house.

The second I pulled into my driveway, Dawn threw her door open and stormed out. She was inside the house the moment I unlocked the front door, and minutes later she was in her bathing suit and on her way to the pool. I followed her and took a seat on a chair while she swam laps fast and hard.

She got out of the pool and walked past me without a word. Minutes later, I found her in the bathroom running a bath.

She lay in the tub, her eyes closed.

"Dawn," I said. "You have to know that I never wanted to hurt you. I wanted to help us. I don't want to hide anything from you. I want to be close with you."

She sunk deeper into the water and kept her eyes shut tight.

"I did what I had to do to support us, but I did a lot more than that too. I am so much more of a person than that label implies. You know that. I'm not the bad choices I made."

Her eyelids flew open. Barely moving, she let her gaze rest on me.

"I cannot believe what you told me," she said. "My own mother." She closed her eyes again as if to make me, make all of this, disappear.

I didn't feel like crying. And I didn't feel like begging her to understand or forgive me. I had always wanted to be as strong as Dawn, and here, for the first time in a long time, I was. I was in my power. I had my voice.

"Dawn," I said, "I worked as a prostitute to make a living. It's what I did; it's not who I am."

Dawn opened her eyes and looked at me. "I cannot talk to you right now—do you get that?"

"I do get that. Take all the time you need." I left her in the bathroom. I wasn't going to push. I had already pushed too much.

That night, Dawn left to stay with her half sister, Stella. It was the start of a long road to healing, but we were on the path.

On Mother's Day, John and I drove to Huntington Beach for brunch at Rocky's place. No one said a word about anything serious. It was a day for just being together—me, John, Dawn, Rocky, and Popeye—all of us, telling stories, laughing, and having a good time.

But then, early that summer, Popeye called. It had been a couple months since I'd told him, and now his anger was surfacing. He began yelling at me for lying to him all these years. He said he was totally shocked and that he couldn't believe his own mom was a prostitute. "It's embarrassing!" he yelled. I was crying as I listened. It was painful to hear how much I'd hurt him, although I was grateful to be present with him so he could express his feelings and his pain. Through my tears, all I could say was, "I get it; I understand how you feel." Popeye was feeling his feelings. I knew he was on the path to healing.

Over the next few months, I wrote twenty letters to my children about the choices I'd made when they were growing up, and when Popeye was ready to listen to them, I brought a letter to read aloud to him every time we got together. I wanted to let him know that the healing is being present with each other—it's listening and learning about each other—and that self-compassion is the antidote to shame. Being open to the experience and available to honor all the feelings that come up is such a healing opportunity.

"Forgiveness is something you do for yourself, sweetheart," I wrote. "Feeling your feelings will help you to heal. We can talk about your thoughts and feelings when you're ready. I'm here whenever you need me."

One day, Popeye surprised me with a question.

"Was your mom a prostitute?" he asked.

I told him that I'd always thought my mother might have slept with men in exchange for a meal, or that maybe they helped her pay the rent or the light bill, but that I had no idea if she did it for money.

The next morning, driving to my office, I heard a radio interview with a man who had been abused by both of his parents when he was little. The interviewer asked the man how he had endured it. "I was used to it," the man said.

I gasped. The man had endured all of that pain because he was used to it?

I pulled over, turned off the engine, and rested my forehead on the steering wheel. My insides were churning, and I wanted to understand why.

An image came to mind. I was little, maybe six years old, and my mother and I were at a bar. The man she was drinking with gave me a few coins to put into the jukebox. I danced while they clapped for me along with the other men seated at the bar.

Another image came to mind. I was older, maybe ten or eleven, and I answered one of my mom's drunken phone calls. She told me she was at a motel and that she would be home in a few days. I told her the refrigerator was empty. I could hear her muffled voice asking someone for money for food if one of her kids came by. She gave me the address of her motel, Steve and I rode our bicycles there, and I took some money from her at the door to her room. I always assumed the man who gave us the money was her boyfriend and that they went to motels for privacy.

All of a sudden, I got it. Those men weren't my mother's boyfriends.

I shuddered. So that was why being a prostitute was easy for me to accept. I was used to it. My mother was a prostitute. An alcoholic and a prostitute.

Separately and together, Popeye and I healed from nearly a lifetime of unasked and unanswered questions. Six months after I told him my truth, he called to say he forgave me. He understood. And he wanted me to know, too, that he didn't think growing up poor was so bad either.

"You always made me feel good about myself, even when you were drinking," he said. "You gave me confidence. I couldn't have started my business without believing I could succeed. I wouldn't be who I am without you."

I had finally told my kids a secret I had carried for twenty-five years. I could finally sleep at night without the lies that blocked me from them.

At Goddess Camp, each of the women had a self-chosen name— Goddess Empowerment, Goddess Heaven on Earth, Goddess Living Love. My name was now Goddess Truth. I wanted to step right into my new name and be the truth of who I was, to be authentic. I set my intention to be seen, to be vulnerable, to be myself, and to be real.

Chapter Twenty-Eight
This Is My Mom

Now that I was focusing on being authentic, I knew I had work to do around my feelings about my mother. I spent some time reflecting on how I'd been ashamed of her, and how I wanted so much for my children to understand and accept me.

I told John about this one night, and he had a great idea.

"All these years, you've been thinking about what was missing for you with your mother. Why don't you try opening up to good memories of her and see what happens?"

Right away, good memories of my mother started coming in. I was very young in them, which meant it was probably before her drinking got bad. I remembered my mother taking me to swimming lessons and to the library for books she would read to me. I remembered going to a weekend camp and my mom volunteering to be one of the parent chaperones, and I remembered playing badminton in our backyard with her. Then I tried to remember good times from later years, but there were none. She was wonderful when she was sober, but it never lasted for more than a few months.

I knew my mother had been arrested a number of times, but I had never known what for. I had always let it go by as part of the crazy chaos. Now I wanted to know.

One morning, I called the police station in an area where we had lived. The officer told me that my mother had been arrested there and in a few other counties in the late fifties and early sixties—six arrests in all. But there was no reason given for the arrests.

I could have jumped through a lot of hoops to find out if I'd really wanted to, but I didn't. What did it matter if my mom was arrested for disturbing the peace in a park when she was drunk or selling her body for sex? What mattered was how I felt about her, and I knew that how I felt about her was up to me.

I went to a drawer of photographs and dug out the one I had of her—a grainy black-and-white from the early fifties. The photo was never framed because it never felt right to have a photograph of her in my home. My mother felt like a stranger to me.

I decided to take my mother's photo with me to lunch that day and really be with her, really see her. I chose one of my favorite restaurants and asked for a booth near the back. I was glad the place was nearly empty, and I propped the photo up in front of a vase of miniature roses. I took a deep breath to center myself, then leaned in on both elbows to get a good look at the picture. It was my mom standing in front of a telephone pole, posing with me and Steve when we were about four and six years old. Greg must have been the photographer that day.

She looked beautiful, tall and slender, dressed in a pencil skirt and a blouse unbuttoned at the neck to show a string of pearls. Her short hair was wavy and dark brown, parted on the right and swept back from her face. The sun was bright and her smile looked easy, her lips parted like she was about to say something to Greg, like, "Honey, hold the camera a little lower. I want the kids in it too." I noticed a slight spark in her eyes, a playful look I recognized in myself and in Rocky. She looked energetic, ready to go. I wished I could say hi to her and hear whatever she might say to me.

"Normal" was what I'd always wanted, and here she was, doing something normal—having her picture taken with her kids. I realized she wanted the best for her children, then and always. She was just doing what she could to survive. I could understand that. She was probably filled with guilt for what she believed was her part in her first daughter's death and she started drinking to numb her pain, ending up an alcoholic in a failed marriage that left her saddled with three kids to raise on her own. Her parents and her brothers and sisters didn't like her choices—divorce and alcoholism—and none of them were there for her.

Looking at that photograph there in the restaurant, I felt really good about my mother for the first time. I saw her not only as my mother but as a woman. I saw myself in her and I liked it, because I liked myself. We were easygoing and nonjudgmental, and we liked to laugh. We had made some similar choices, not all of them healthy for us or for our children. I forgave her. I forgave the both of us.

"Wow," I whispered, "this is my mom." It was the strangest feeling. I repeated it over and over: "This is my mom."

After lunch, I went straight to a camera shop and had the photo copied and cropped and made into a larger image of just my mom's face. I framed it and placed it on my vanity, next to a photo of Joy.

Later that evening, alone with my mother's energy and her photo by my side, I brought my laptop to bed. Continuing to tell the truth to my children had become especially important to me, and I wanted to keep the healing process in motion. I wrote this letter from my heart, with the intention that through understanding, we could grow even closer:

To my three children,

When I was twenty-three years old, I wanted to have children more than anything in the world. I thought I would raise you perfectly and that we would have a perfect life together with so much love and everything I didn't have when I was growing up. Little did I know that I was still a little girl myself and that I was in no way ready to raise children. I brought you into this life not prepared to give you what you needed.

I was lost in so many ways. I was an alcoholic. I had phobias, panic attacks, deep insecurities, and feelings of unworthiness, shame, and of not being good enough. I was way out of balance and immature. I never felt like I fit in or that I belonged. I didn't think I was smart enough, good enough, or lovable.

And at the time, I didn't even know these things about myself. They were buried deep inside of me. I was damaged by the experience that I endured being raised by a mother who was just as damaged and out of balance as I was. And I believe she, like me, didn't know it either when she decided to have children.

I know that I put you all in terrible situations, confusing you like I'd been confused. I can now take responsibility for forcing you out of situations that must have felt good, safe, and normal, only to thrust you into situations that were horrible and unpredictable. You needed to feel loved, safe, and secure. Instead, because I was a product of the same abuse, neglect, and shame, you were victims of the reckless behavior that I had developed over the years.

I have not been the mother that I thought I would or

could be. There were times when I thought I did a wonderful job, and then I'd do something to mess that all up.

I know what it feels like to be ashamed of your mother. I know what it feels like to want to get away from all of it. And I know what it can do to you. I know how it can destroy your spirit and make you question where you come from and who you were meant to be. I know how it can change you, how it can damage you, causing you to want to reach for things to numb your pain and find ways to escape whenever you can.

I believe we all have a calling in life and a gift to bring to the world. Over the past twelve years, I have been able to do a lot of healing with the help and love of therapists, teachers, and a remarkable community of friends.

I was able to grow and heal, and I continue to grow and heal with the love and support that I have from John, who is also my spiritual partner. Spiritual partners are equals at the soul level, although the personalities may be different. Our purpose as spiritual partners is to support each other in our spiritual growth and healing.

I know each of you will need to heal in your own way and in your own time. I know there is no way to rush this. Just recently, I was finally able to return to love and understanding with my own mother. For me this was enormously healing.

Whatever path you take, whatever timing you choose, I want you to know that I get you. I get your pain, your shame, your anger and frustration.

Now, when you need me to be there for you, I can. I can help you from a place of love, understanding, and compassion. I won't try to rush this in any way. Just know that I'm here for you whenever you need me.

I know that, through it all, we still have love. And I
thank God that, through it all, each one of you has found
love in your life.

With deep compassion and love,
Mom

One night not long after I wrote the letter, John called me into
the living room.

"I've been smelling something really sweet in here for the past
couple of days," he said. "I can't figure out what it is." He pointed to
a place about four feet above the carpet between the coffee table and
the armoire. "It's really strong right there. Can you smell it?"

I went over to the place where he smelled it, and sure enough,
there was a fruity, candy smell.

"It's Life Savers!" I cried. "It's my mom! My mother bought me
Life Savers all the time when I was little."

"Well, I guess she's still bringing you Life Savers," he said.

Once again, I was awed by the power of the spirit world.

Moments later, while sitting on a chair in the dining room, John
smelled the sweet smell again. "You're not going to believe this," he
said, "but come here." He pointed to his nose.

I went up close to John and sniffed, and sure enough, the smell
was right there on the tip of his nose. I laughed, squeezing him tight.
"My mother thinks I got it right with you, right on the nose!"

I'd let my mother back into my life, and she showed up in ways
she never could before. I recognized that she had done the best she
could with what she had. I had longed for my mother for years, and it
had finally come to an end. I had her if I forgave her.

And I had finally forgiven her.

Chapter Twenty-Nine
Full Circle

After a lifetime of doing our own healing work, John and I began counseling individuals and couples within our community. It became the most rewarding experience.

The Goddess Camps had expanded to include men, and John and I hosted some of these God/Goddess Camps at our home in Encino. I loved seeing John and the other men get the rich, delicious experience I had been getting for so long. Goddess Camp gave me a sense of belonging and connection. I realized I was no better or worse than anybody else. We were more alike than we were different. For me, that was the most important lesson because I'd always thought everybody was better than me. I passed on what I had learned on my journey to freedom: positive self-talk, a daily gratitude practice, meditation, prayer, and chakra balancing. What a joy it was to finally share my wisdom and experience with those willing to do the work.

John and I had done tremendous work together, and we were ready to take it into the world. For some time we had talked about creating a program called "Transform with the Tierneys," and in 2014, we were ready to start.

We held the events in our home every two months and brought in some of our friends as facilitators, bringing together the young and the old, providing a safe space for everyone to share their stories and experience true intimacy. We offered a chance for interrelatedness that wasn't possible at twelve-step meetings. We promoted and practiced verbalizing thoughts and feelings, getting in our power, setting boundaries, and speaking up for ourselves. We used eye-gazing techniques and other nonsexual intimacy practices. We used healthy dating plans, which included becoming friends with another person before falling into the "in love" trap, the fantasy. We promoted the constant practice of self-love, acceptance, and forgiveness so that we could love, accept, and forgive others.

We endearingly called our attendees "Transformers," and we established the following as the Transform Mission Statement:

This is a safe and sacred space.
We are seen, we are heard, we matter. We are loved.
We let go of who we were so we may become who we were meant to be.
We move toward wholeness. We create our best selves.
We face our fears; we walk through the fire. We know that everything serves us, everything is a gift.
We serve a higher purpose. With love, forgiveness, and acceptance.
We heal together; we grow together.
We look back over our shoulders and honor how far we've come.
With so much love and gratitude, we allow and receive the blessings of our newfound happiness, joy, and freedom.
Together, we TRANSFORM.

Those who came to Transform got the chance to feel that they were not alone. They were understood and were in a safe place to release the shame or the negativity that had been hidden in their secrets for so long. They all had their own stories, trauma, and pain.

Many had endured horrible experiences of sexual abuse and had lived in torment. Some had been involved in prostitution, on both sides of the exchange. No matter the story, they were all trying to escape the pain and were acting out in various ways, through different addictions. Though the stories were different, we could all relate to one another and connect, in a way we never knew we craved.

John and I supported our Transformers in their dreams, reminding them not to let anyone tell them they couldn't do something. If they could dream it, they could have it, as long as they believed and didn't let go of their dream. We understood that the advice people give is based on what they believe *they* can or can't do—and that these limitations don't universally apply to everyone. We helped to empower our Transformers, reminding them, "There is only one unique you." We told them, "If you want something, go for it!" I encouraged them to understand that it was none of their business what other people thought about them. I would say, "Other people's thoughts are only about *them*. They are *their* thoughts, *their* opinions, *their* beliefs, *their* prejudices, *their* ideas of what is right or wrong. The only thing that matters is what *you* think about yourself."

Word spread about the benefits of Transform with the Tierneys, and John and I felt richly rewarded. We were not only helping others but also feeling recognized, valued, and needed ourselves. Lives were changing for the better, and it felt so good to make a difference.

* * *

Meanwhile, Dawn had been going through a rough time. I wanted to be there for her and comfort her, so I bought a plane ticket and stayed with her for a few days.

What a mistake.

I didn't know what was harder, being a mother or having one.

I was walking on eggshells. I tried to comfort her, but I couldn't say a single word right. My desire for closeness had desperation about it, and she hated it. We both hated it.

After three unbearable days, I went home, and then I called her to apologize for how awkward it had been. I was surprised by her response—she told me that we didn't need to be in a perfect relationship. We could be angry with each other, and it was okay. She could feel angry without it ending her love for me.

Her response reminded me of something I'd learned about her when she was a young teen: Dawn knew how to say what she did or didn't want with no apology. She was confident and seemed to have a great sense of self. She said what was on her mind. She wasn't a people pleaser like I had been. When I saw that strength in her, I'd often think, *I want to be just like Dawn when I grow up.*

I felt relieved that I finally had permission to let go of needing a perfect mother-daughter relationship. I knew it wouldn't happen overnight, but I was committed to making it happen. I wanted to be close to Dawn more than anything in the world.

I finally understood that we don't see things as they are; we see things as *we* are. By letting go of the expectations in my relationship with her, I was able to experience a different kind of mother-daughter relationship. I was accepting of Dawn as she was, and I stopped needing her to be anything but my daughter. If she had been the daughter I'd once thought I wanted, I wouldn't have become the woman I was now proud to be. I wouldn't have had half the drive I had to heal our family. Not a third. I could now see how awful it had been for Dawn growing up, seeing me with boyfriend after boyfriend. Dawn had needed my attention, and I had given it all away to the men I was involved with instead of my own daughter.

I'd been so driven by my desperation for Dawn's love and

acceptance that sometimes I'd overshare. When I did, Dawn would say, "Boundaries, Mom." By requesting that I honor her boundaries, I eventually learned to set my own. I no longer needed to be anyone but myself around her, and I no longer needed her approval. I mustered up the courage and called her often to practice being myself, not worrying about what she would or wouldn't want me to say or what she liked or didn't like about me. I found myself as I began to speak from my heart. I hadn't been able to see the wonderful, loving daughter she'd been all these years, but I finally realized that all along, she'd been right in front of me. I felt pure love!

For my seventy-third birthday, I received the most beautiful card from Dawn. The outside said, *You're a Great Mom.* On the inside, Dawn wrote:

> Mom, you really have instilled a confidence and love in me that I'm very thankful for. I pass on so many of the things you taught me to my kids. I'm very lucky to have such a loving, accepting mom.
>
> You've always accepted everyone no matter who they are, and I don't think it has been until now that I realized what a gift that was for me. I think I assumed all parents taught their kids that. You really love people for who they are and that is magnificent.
>
> I love you. Happy birthday.
>
> Love, Dawn

In October of 2021, John and I stayed for a week with Dawn; her husband, Sean; and my two adorable grandchildren. We had the most beautiful time enjoying one another's company. We shared the warmest hugs as I felt Dawn's love and acceptance. I could see how loving and especially close she was with her children, and I admired how she made herself available to them. Dawn is the mother I always wanted to be. She's a wonderful mother.

And like Dawn, Popeye is also a great parent. He's very present and loving with his daughter. He is the dad I wish I could have had. On top of it all, he's always there for me when I need him. I cherish the time I get to spend with him; his wife, Kelly; and my sweet granddaughter.

I'm incredibly proud of Rocky as well. He is a spiritual man with a heart of gold and a passion for being of service. Through his business, he offers support for people healing from their drug addictions and transitioning into healthy, sober lifestyles. He's made a wonderful life with his spiritual partner, Rachel. Rocky makes everyone he's with—including me—feel like they're the most important person in the world.

I am blown away by the amazing lives my children have created, considering everything I put them through while they were growing up, and yet at the same time I'm not surprised because they've always been such good people, and I'm proud of the fact that I can look up to my kids and learn from them. I always believed they would be successful.

* * *

Transform with the Tierneys has given me the opportunity to give my energy to those who need it—and I had no idea that I would be one of those people who needed it. Through our program, I finally got in touch with my own feelings, and, through deep cries, my childhood wounds began to heal. Now, as I look back over my shoulder at the traumatic events in my life, I realize that I have gained so much wisdom—post-traumatic wisdom.

I spent my entire life trying to be perfect. I thought that if I was perfect, people would love me, that I'd be enough. But I now know that perfect doesn't exist. I want more than anything to be authentic. To relax. I'm ready to be real. I've started to practice; I have years of habits to break. It's hard practicing to be seen. It's scary, but I'm on the path. I'm learning to have the courage to be imperfect, to have compassion for myself. I'm ready to be vulnerable. When I listen to people who are vulnerable, I really see them; I feel the connection, the intimacy. I realize it's their vulnerability that makes them beautiful, and I want that!

I can own the actions I've taken in my life, and there's no shame it. Today, I am sober, loving, patient, and nonjudgmental. When faced with a difficult situation, I've learned to choose love over fear. I treat others with the kindness, understanding, and goodness that I saw in my own mother when she was sober. Through forgiveness, I have finally given up hope that the past could've been any different. My mom was always off *doing* something, so I thought that was love. I've realized that *being* with my children is love. They need *me*, my *time*. I am present with them now, and I can honor all their feelings. That is the healing.

I have finally healed the pain of the past and am now creating wonderful new experiences with my children and grandchildren.

I am finally the mother I was meant to be.

Acknowledgments

M y beloved John: Thank you for your constant support with my book and for listening to me read it over and over again. Thank you for cheering me on and for being the best guy I have ever known!

Charlene: Thank you for your deep understanding and for getting me like only my beautiful spirit daughter could. Thank you for modeling how to feel my feelings, which allowed me to write from a deeper place, and thank you for your magnificent writing, for being the best editor, and for your dedication and love for this book.

Josh: You encouraged me to feel more of my feelings and to add them to this book, knowing it would make it a deeper and more insightful story, and you were right. Thank you for your love and your caring support.

Joy: Thank you for believing in my ability to write this book, for supporting me, and for instilling a confidence in me so I could tell my truth with no apology. Thank you for changing my life!

God/Goddess Community: Thank you for seeing me, for going deep, for all the sharing and processing, and for so much fun. Each one of you helped lift me to my highest self and prepared me to write this book—it's been a long road, but it's finally here!

Transformers: Thank you for joining me and John at our retreats and for having the courage to tell your stories. Your truths. Because of you I can share the healing benefits of Transform with the world.

Mom: You told me I didn't have to be like everybody else, and for that I am so grateful. That message gave me the freedom to be who I am. It's because of you I am able to tell my story and help others.

Kara: It means the world to have an amazing friend like you. You've supported me every step of the way, including being my "acting coach" while you so generously let me record my book in your private studio. Thank you!

Freda: Thank you for letting me read to you and for loving my book so much. You are the most present person I've ever known. Thank you for reminding me to take the time to appreciate how far I've come. I cherish our amazing connection.

Jonathon: Thank you, my dear friend, for writing the very special book *Self-Love*. It shows the importance of loving ourselves from the inside out, which helped me be a better writer.

Miriam: Thank you from the bottom of my heart for showing up for me the way you did and for your thorough reading and thoughtful suggestions. I hold you in the highest regard.

Jamye: Because of your love and guidance during our therapy sessions, I was able to move through some painful, stuck energy. You offered me a new perspective which allowed me to feel what I hadn't been able to. That was enormously healing. Thank you!

Oprah: When you taught me about spirituality, it gave me a deep sense of awareness about who I am and why I'm here. Because of you, I've learned to believe in myself, which enabled me to write this book and tell my truth. Thank you!

About the Author

© Mary Lou Sandler, 3 cubed studios, LLC

Patty Tierney worked as a prostitute to support her three children for seventeen years. After getting sober at forty-six years old, her life began to change, and she eventually began a career in caregiving. In 2005 she started her first caregiving company, which she successfully ran for ten years before selling it and shifting her focus to being a private caregiver.

Patty and her husband, John, together host retreats called Transform with the Tierneys, through which they provide a safe space for people to share their stories and practice self-love, acceptance, and forgiveness. For more about Transform, see www.transformwiththetierneys.com.

Today, Patty's three adult children are thriving and successful, and she adores her three grandchildren. She and John live happily in Encino, California; they are best friends, and they love being together. When she's not caregiving, hosting Transform, or spending time with family, Patty keeps herself busy with her passion for writing. For more about what she's working on now or for information on private one-on-one counseling or coaching with Patty, visit www.pattytierney.com.

About Children of the Night

A portion of the proceeds of this book will go to Children of the Night.

Children of the Night is a privately funded nonprofit organization established in 1979 with the specific purpose to provide intervention in the lives of children who are sexually exploited and vulnerable to or involved in prostitution and pornography.

Since their inception in 1979, all Children of the Night programs have been exclusively **<u>funded by private donations</u>** from foundations, corporations, and individuals.

For more info: www.childrenofthenight.org

SELECTED TITLES FROM SHE WRITES PRESS

She Writes Press is an independent publishing company founded to serve women writers everywhere. Visit us at www.shewritespress.com.

Fetish Girl: A Memoir of Sex, Domination, and Motherhood by Bella LaVey. $16.95, 978-1-63152-435-6

A kinky roller coaster ride through addiction, violence, motherhood, sex, and the creation of Evil Kitty, Bella LaVey's larger-than-life dominatrix persona, this singular memoir is the story of a woman attracted to extremes who is willing to go to great lengths to uncover and make peace with her true nature.

Don't Call Me Mother: A Daughter's Journey from Abandonment to Forgiveness by Linda Joy Myers. $16.95, 978-1-93831-402-5

Linda Joy Myers's story of how she transcended the prisons of her childhood by seeking—and offering—forgiveness for her family's sins.

Bowing to Elephants: Tales of a Travel Junkie by Mag Dimond $16.95, 978-1-63152-596-4

Mag Dimond, an unloved girl from San Francisco, becomes a travel junkie to avoid the fate of her narcissistic, alcoholic mother—but everywhere she goes, she's haunted by memories of her mother's neglect, and by a hunger to find out who she is, until she finds peace and her authentic self in the refuge of Buddhist practice.

Finding Venerable Mother: A Daughter's Spiritual Quest to Thailand by Cindy Rasicot. $16.95, 978-1-63152-702-9

In midlife, Cindy travels halfway around the world to Thailand and unexpectedly discovers a Thai Buddhist nun who offers her the unconditional love and acceptance her own mother was never able to provide. This soulful and engaging memoir reminds readers that when we go forward with a truly open heart, faith, forgiveness, and love are all possible.